THE DON'T SWEAT GUIDE
FOR COUPLES

THE DON'T SWEAT GUIDE
FOR COUPLES

Ways to Be More Intimate, Loving and Stress-Free in Your Relationship

By the Editors of Don't Sweat Press
Foreword by Richard Carlson, Ph.D.,
author of the bestselling *Don't Sweat the Small Stuff*

New York

ISBN 978-0-7868-8720-0

Hyperion books are available for special promotions, premiums, or corporate
training. For details contact Michael Rentas, Proprietary Markets, Hyperion,
77 West 66th Street, 12th floor, New York, New York 10023, or call 212-456-0133.

FIRST EDITION

10 9 8 7 6 5 4 3

Contents

Foreword   11

1. Remember the One That You Fell For   15

2. Read the Same Book   17

3. Be a Friend   19

4. Sing in the Shower   21

5. Turn Ruts into Rituals   23

6. Wait for the End of the Sentence   25

7. Learn Sign Language   27

8. Practice Praise   29

9. Share the Sandbox   31

10. Remember That Pigeonholes Are for the Birds!   33

11. Expect Surprises   35

12. Appreciate the Benefits of a Doubt   37

13. Study the "Who's Who" of Living Together   39

14. Find a Room of Your Own   41

15. Lose the Laundry List   43

16. Appreciate the Present   45

17. Expect to Learn   47

18. Speak Your Mind—No One Will Read It   49

19. Be the Bright Spot in Your Partner's Day   51

20. Know Your Limits   53

21. Have an Adventure Together   55

22. Give When It's Least Expected   57

23. Turn Differences into Complements   59

24. Lengthen Your Fuse   61

25. Love with an Open Hand   63

26. Cherish the Child in Your Partner   65

27. Try on a Different Pair of Shoes   67

28. Live the Life That You Always Hoped to Have   69

29. Build Bridges Instead of Walls   71

30. Emphasize the Estimable   73

31. Fly in Formation   75

32. Choose Where You Are   77

33. Forget to Keep Score   79

34. Make the First Move   81

35. Learn to Breathe   83

36. Think with Your Heart, Feel with Your Head   85

37. Aim for the Extraordinary   87

38. Extend Your Reach   89

39. Know Who You Are   91

40. Be a Cheerleader Instead of a Critic   93

41. Assume Nothing but the Best   95

42. Create an Atmosphere of Tolerance   97

43. Don't Pick the Scabs   99

44. Laugh Easily   101

45. Learn the Art of the Strategic Retreat   103

46. Lend a Hand Once a Day   105

47. Be the Partner That You'd Like to Have   107

48. Find Reasons to Say Thank You   109

49. Bend When the Wind Blows   111

50. Savor Every Bite   113

51. Take No Prisoners   115

52. Divide the Labor   117

53. Take a Break   119

54. Change the Scenery   121

55. Give More Than Necessary   123

56. Banish the Bogeymen   125

57. Be Your Own Best Friend   127

58. Honor Your Secret Knowledge   129

59. Throw a Snowball   131

60. Renew Your Promises   133

61. Define Common Space   135

62. Take a Bird's-Eye View   137

63. Plant a Tree   139

64. Retrain the Knee-Jerk Reactions   141

65. Be a Haven   143

66. Keep the Back Door Open   145

67. Talk with Your Hands   147

68. Don't Sweat the Tides   149

69. Do What You Love   151

70. Honor Your Partner's Roots   153

71. Turn Down the Volume   155

72. Admit It!   157

73. Delete "Failure" from Your Vocabulary   159

74. Listen with Your *Other* Ears   161

75. Tend to Your Business   163

76. Institute the "Time-Out" Strategy   165

77. Be Ready for Bright Ideas   167

78. Nurture Your Body   169

79. Nourish Your Spirit   171

80. Exercise Your Intellect   173

81. Share Your Offspring   175

82. Honor Your Own Roots   177

83. Maintain Some Mystery   179

84. Promote Pillow Talk   181

85. Make Meals into Dates   183

86. Once a Month, Trade Jobs   185

87. Volunteer Together   187

88. Sort, Dispose, and Donate   189

89. When in Doubt, Make Up   191

90. Listen Between the Lines   193

91. Test Your Judgment   195

92. Articulate Your "Ouches"   197

93. Resist Humor at Your Partner's Expense   199

94. Remember Love   201

95. Believe in the Power of One   203

96. Go Mountain Climbing   205

97. Delete the Negative   207

Foreword

Being part of a couple, in a committed relationship, is one of life's greatest treasures. That is, if it's a good one! All kidding aside, being a couple is a true gift. It provides the opportunity for love, companionship, friendship, family, and security. But, no matter how great your relationship may be, there is probably going to be at least some stress associated with it. The very fact that two people are together lends itself to some inherent issues—the need to compromise, forgive, accept differences, and sacrifice. Sometimes you disagree or have different wants, needs, and desires. You may have different goals and priorities, and must deal with each other's issues and moods.

The editors of Don't Sweat Press have done a beautiful job in creating a guide to overcome much of the stress usually associated with being a couple. *The Don't Sweat Guide for Couples* is a simple, practical collection of strategies designed to give you and your partner tools to work together better, let go of things easier, and focus your attention on the love you have for each other. Often in our relationships, we use our minds in self-defeating or negative ways that encourage our love to drift away. Becoming aware of this tendency—and the power of our own thinking—is a magical tool for enhancing the love we have for our partners. It helps us eliminate any negative habits that may have crept into our relationships.

I encourage you to read this book alone, or side by side with your partner. Either way, I'm guessing you're going to learn some very helpful tools.

My relationship with my wife, Kris, is such an important part of my life. The two of us are committed to doing all we can to enhance the quality of our own relationship. Many of the ideas in this book resonated in our hearts, as I hope they will in yours.

Thank you for being committed to the quality of your relationship. I hope this book is of tremendous service to you and to your partner.

Treasure the Gift of Love,
Richard Carlson
Pleasant Hill, CA, June 2001

THE DON'T SWEAT GUIDE
FOR COUPLES

1.

Remember the One
That You Fell For

There is a period close to the beginning of most long-term relationships when we're so swept up in the excitement of the chemistry of being in love that we don't mind the things in our partners that will later become ingredients for stress. Most of us eventually get over this rosy view. But in the process of descending from the heights of infatuation, we can sometimes move too far in the opposite direction. We are no longer blinded by love, and have to grapple with the reality of another flesh-and-blood person. It's a natural, necessary, and healthy part of love, but it feels like a loss, and it causes pain.

There's no easy cure for the stresses of life as a couple. But your view of the person with whom you share those stresses can go a long way toward affecting how important you allow the stresses to become. When you remember the hows, whys, and wherefores of falling in love with your partner, you maintain a sympathetic, appreciative perspective of that person.

The process of remembering the one that you fell for starts within you. Think back to your first glimpse of your partner. Remember the details of your partner's personality, appearance, preferences, and habits. Think about how those aspects affected you when they were all new to you, and remember what you found attractive.

Remembering the one that you fell for can also be a two-way street. Take walks with your partner down "Memory Lane." In the early days of romance, you shared some powerful emotions and exciting times. Recalling them together can bring them back into focus and even spark new life in the here and now. Celebrate special occasions by returning to old haunts that have significance for you as a couple. Pull out old photographs, laugh about happy times, and plan activities that you used to enjoy doing together. Don't seek to recreate the past, but let it feed a richer experience in the present.

In short, make your shared history a powerful tool for a happier, more satisfying life with your partner. In the process, you'll free up room for a love that continues to grow and deepen.

2.

Read the Same Book

It takes time for people to grow apart. It is the culmination of hundreds of separate choices made without reference to the health of the relationship. The partners go their own ways in activities that are most engaging, and save the mundane things for togetherness. The relationship can become associated with boredom and tedium.

In the same way, it takes time for people to build a strong foundation of mutual growth and vitality. This is meaningful time that a couple chooses to spend together in pursuits that are stimulating and challenging. Growing together instead of apart requires that you share life's learning curves with your partner, day after day, in a variety of ways.

Perhaps your partner plays golf, runs, skis, or boats. You may not have any background in these activities, but you can certainly learn. You may not have the physical ability or find that an activity doesn't grow on you. But you can appreciate what it takes, and be an active supporter in a variety of ways. Your partner's area of strength may be intellectual; it may be artistic; it may lie in home maintenance. Just participating alongside your partner gives you the opportunity to learn new skills and appreciate more about your loved one.

By the same token, share your own strengths. It may seem easier and more efficient to avoid the explanations and coaching time involved in sharing your strengths with your partner, but ease and efficiency don't necessarily feed mutual growth.

If you're both readers, read the same book, either separately or aloud to one another. Talk about your reactions to it. The content of the book becomes a shared experience that draws you together. Take up a new activity that neither of you has tried or mastered already. Sign up for dancing lessons or join a bicycling group. If you enjoy travel and have the means, plan trips to places neither of you have visited. If you're social types, make new friends in common.

With each choice to learn and grow together, you build a history of mutual support and an inventory of engaging activities that bond you and make you interesting to one another. By comparison, the things that lead to stress and friction will be boring. You won't want to expend any energy on them.

3.

Be a Friend

Life partners do not necessarily treat one another as the friends they could or should be. There can be many reasons for this, but the net result is that these people have better friendships outside of their relationship than they do with their loved one.

It need not be this way. You can change an unsatisfying status quo. To begin, be the kind of friend to your partner that you would like to have. Stand close in support when times are tough, lend a shoulder to cry on in circumstances of sorrow, and offer a sympathetic ear when life is confusing. Congratulate your partner on success, and extend the benefit of a doubt when you don't understand what's going on. Maintain and express your confidence in your partner. In the act of *being* a friend, you will earn the right to *have* a friend in your partner.

You must also teach your partner how to be your friend in romance. Find a non-accusatory a way of communicating. Rather than expressing yourself in terms of "You never... " or "I wish you would…" focus on "It would mean a lot to me if…" or "One of the needs I have is…" In this way, you acknowledge that the needs are yours, and you allow your partner to make a gift of friendship to you.

When you extend friendship to your partner and you are rebuffed, you may want to take another look at your act of friendship. Are you focusing on what is important to your partner, or are you stubbornly offering only what you feel like offering? Are you treating your partner the way that you treat other close friends? Finally, have you taken into consideration any anger or pain that may be getting in the way? Sometimes the forward motion of a friendship is stalled because some necessary apologies were never made.

There's little in life that adds as much joy as a solid, supportive friendship with the person you've chosen as a partner. If you express what friendship means to you and pursue it explicitly in the context of friendship, you can move past the petty reactions that have grown out of wishing for it. Concentrate on attacking the problem at the source of the trouble, and the symptoms will take care of themselves.

4.

Sing in the Shower

A mong the people you know are those who have had to face a
seemingly disproportionate number of woes in their lives, but
who continue to have an upbeat, optimistic attitude. Then there
are others who seem to have a special radar for the negative, who
have problems even on the sunniest days, and who will readily
pinpoint who or what is to blame for what ails them.

The difference between these people has to do with their
attitude and perspective; what you might think of as the "climate
within." Optimistic, upbeat people develop a way of viewing life,
with all its potential problems, that inclines them to accept the
unchangeable and seek positive solutions.

And that is the point. Regardless of what it may take to move
in the direction of deeper joy and optimism, it begins with a
conscious desire to feel and be happy. It does *not* depend on what
life throws in your path, and it does not depend on your partner. It
is yours alone, and it can be brought to bear upon whatever you

encounter. It can be as simple as singing in the shower, or as complicated as sorting out the pains and sorrows you've held onto for a lifetime.

Any number of options are open to you in pursuit of a positive attitude. Consider, for example, the amount and quality of time you devote to the life of your spirit. Reflection, prayer, service to others, and worship are ways to help you find a joy-filled place to stand in times of stress.

Your emotional well-being is also tied to your physical well-being. Many people have found that a good mood is one of the side effects of regular exercise. When they pay attention to a balanced way of eating and drinking, they have more energy and enthusiasm.

Also consider how you treat your mind. What kind of "food" do you feed it? A steady diet of violent or negative entertainment does little to sustain an attitude of hope. Likewise, any quantity of time spent in the company of chronic complainers, gossips, or doom-and-gloom mongers will have its influence on your inner climate. Choose your mental food carefully. Sprinkle a liberal dose of uplifting experiences into your life through what you listen to, read, watch, and participate in. And balance the time you spend with negative people with those who follow a more positive path.

5.

Turn Ruts into Rituals

A rut is a path so well-worn that it makes change very difficult. When you travel that path, you go in the same direction, in the same manner as the last time. You may glimpse another way to travel the path or change your destination, but the rut makes change just problematic enough so that you're tempted not to make the effort. The result is a sense of let-down, of opportunity missed. Out of that grow regret and self-recrimination. Even worse, you may be so used to your rut that you cease to see alternatives.

Ruts don't happen to us. We choose to fall into those patterns and perpetuate them without questioning their value to our lives. It is not creating and maintaining patterns, per se, that allows ruts to wreak their havoc. Instead, it's failing to consider *why* we're traveling the same path in the same way and neglecting to decide whether another way would serve better.

A rut may be a train of thought, a habit of response, or a pattern of behavior. If you go without examining it for too long, you risk shortchanging the well-being of your closest relationship. A rut loses some of its power when you realize that you're in it. With that recognition comes the opportunity to rethink your chosen pattern, change it, or transform its effect on you.

Take, for example, the daily habit of reading the newspaper at the breakfast table. Many partners resent having to stare across a coffee cup at a page of newsprint. From that irritation sprouts any number of others, simply because the day begins with a shared behavior—shared by one reading silently, and the other not addressing it constructively—that is ultimately damaging.

Reading the newspaper at the breakfast table can enhance a couple's time together if they consciously make that choice. Discussing what they've read and making frequent eye contact can transform an off-putting habit into food for mutual enjoyment and growth. A routine of watching a certain television show or video together can become a cherished ritual.

What turns ruts into rituals is a conscious *shared* decision. What keeps rituals from devolving into ruts is the willingness to stay conscious and keep choosing.

6.

Wait for the End
of the Sentence

Few skills are more important to the quality of a relationship than the skill of being a good listener. The first step in good listening is making a conscious effort to pay attention. Human beings can think far more quickly than they can talk. When your partner is speaking, you take in what is said with time to spare. This can allow your mind to wander, and you may be distracted to the point where you stop listening. Furthermore, because you are thinking faster than the other person can speak, you may anticipate where a subject is headed. You may finish the next thought for your partner—either literally or mentally. You fail to absorb the actual message, and a lack of communication results.

Good listening also depends on your physical behavior. Watch what your partner is saying with gestures, facial expressions, and posture. Make eye contact. At the same time, communicate with your own gestures, expressions, and posture that you are "with" your partner. Nod attentively, and avoid crossing your arms or shaking your head. The same physical gestures that make you *look* like you're listening can actually help you to listen more effectively.

Never assume that you know what's coming next, or that you know all that there is to know. Like all people, your partner is constantly developing in ways that can only be discovered by paying close attention in moments of conversation. If you don't wait to hear the end of a sentence, you may miss the changes occurring. You miss the opportunity to know more about the one that you love.

Listen without passing judgment. The quickest way to shut someone down is to criticize and correct instead of hearing her out. Make a point of clarifying what you're hearing. Be thoughtful before you turn the conversation to concerns of your own. Sometimes in the interest of showing empathy, we answer revelations from our partners with those of our own. This can create mutual understanding, but if it happens too often or too quickly, it can communicate a relative disinterest in the other person. Focusing entirely on what your partner is saying and giving your partner time to finish speaking show that you are listening carefully.

7.

Learn Sign Language

It's a fact of intimate life that we know our partner's preferences, frustrations, and foibles. Some of these private idiosyncrasies have public ramifications, and we sometimes need to communicate something about them in front of others. Perhaps one of you tends to talk too loudly. Maybe one of you wants to leave a gathering, or one of you needs rescuing from a bore. Whatever the issue, communicating so that others notice can be awkward and embarrassing.

One effective way of offsetting this is to invent a collection of signals that allow you to communicate privately as a couple. For example, suppose your partner sometimes dips a sleeve in the food on the dinner table. Agree as a pair that if your partner needs a cleanup reminder, you will say, "Did you happen to bring a handkerchief?" Someone else might tug at an earlobe while making eye contact to indicate that the teeth need cleaning. The particulars of the signals are far less important than the fact of them. The ability to communicate without speaking allows you and your partner to be allies in ways that are yours alone, while honoring your privacy in public venues.

Such a solution requires sensitivity and communication. When you first become aware of a situation, it may help to think before you speak. In public, if you're up against something that you've never handled before, it might be a good idea to stay silent and discuss it later. Admit that you didn't know what to say, but for the future, you'd like to know what your partner would prefer. After the issue actually comes up and you put your plans into action, double-check that you both are happy with the results.

Attention to intimate communication when you and your partner are among others can forestall hurt feelings, humiliation, and subsequent blowups. You're dealing with the source of stress instead of the symptoms, and in the process, forging a stronger bond.

8.

Practice Praise

At first, when we form relationships with other people, we tend to focus more on the positive. But over time, as we gain more experience with a partner's negative traits, our focus shifts. We see that our partners are the same mix of positive and negative that we are ourselves. What we perceive in our partners as negative often threatens our own sense of well-being and comfort, so we want to fix it or make it go away to feel safe and happy again.

Sadly, the natural defense mechanism that makes us see and react to the negative may eventually obscure the positive. The good in our partners that we once noticed fades into the background. Our comments become a stream of worries, indictments, and complaints. Our partners begin to wonder if we even still love them. In response, they erect defenses. As a result, we reinforce the negative in one another instead of the positive.

This process can be reversed. You can help yourself at the outset by being honest about yourself. Most people know that they have faults. That can be a comfort as you view your partner's faults. It should remind you that you won't find someone who is fault-free. You have the potential for empathy and forgiveness for someone who has faults, as you do. Knowing that you need these emotions to successfully navigate your course should help you accept that your partner does, too.

Having reckoned with the negative, you can free yourself to return to the positive. Make up your mind to identify and carefully consider at least one admirable trait or quality in your mate every day for a week. At the end of a week, take the opportunity to share what you've been thinking with your partner about just one of the traits. It can be as simple as, "I just wanted to tell you how much I appreciate this about you."

Of course, you may not have to work that hard to notice the positive aspects of the one you love. Perhaps the more pressing need is remembering to offer words of praise. Many times, we take for granted that our partners know what we appreciate in them. In reality, most of us need a lot of feedback about the good in us and about our worthy actions, especially from our partners.

9.

Share the Sandbox

It's amazing how otherwise mature, reasonable adults can be so childish as they deal with shared living space. The neatnik goes to battle over the pack rat's piles of "junk." The hospital-corner expert tears out his hair over lopsided bedcovers. And the nature lover weeps over her mate's overzealous shrub-trimming.

Most often, these matters are products of personal styles, upbringing, and habit. Yet when they exist between people whose basic inclinations are opposite, they have the potential to create tensions.

Remember the days when the biggest problem you had was how to share toys with your friends in the sandbox? Maybe you drew a line down the middle of the box and said, "This is my side, that is yours." Maybe you made a pile of toys in the middle and took turns selecting which ones you would use.

As cohabiting adults, recognize that you may not be dealing with right and wrong as much as difference. Where, after all, is it written that being neat is morally superior to being messy? Or that shrubs should be pruned to an organic rather than a formal shape? Loving partners deserve a strong dose of perspective from each other and an appreciation for the ridiculous. They also deserve genuine respect from one another.

So let's return to the playground. Admit to each other that the differences that arise over mutual housekeeping can irritate and annoy you. Then put your sense of perspective into play. "Look," you may say, "this keeps coming up between us and makes us act silly. I love you too much to waste emotional energy on this. What can we do about it?" With the issue acknowledged but placed firmly within the larger framework of a loving relationship, you have a terrific starting place for compromise and cooperation.

Remember that your mate has as much right to want a home that feels comfortable as you do. If you have real differences in what makes you comfortable, you may have to assign certain spaces that you don't share. You will have to respect one another enough to give each other due consideration as you work out compromises. The reward is a home atmosphere that demonstrates the love that you share.

10.

Remember That Pigeonholes
Are for the Birds!

A pigeonhole, by definition, confines. If you're a pigeon looking for a site to nest, such confinement spells safety. But if you're a human being living with another human being, a pigeonhole implies the loss of hope and trust, the inability to grow and heal, shrinking love, and increasing isolation. People don't belong in pigeonholes, and placing someone there can be hurtful. Relatively unimportant irritations can become major stumbling blocks when two partners stubbornly stuff each other into pigeonholes and reject the possibility of change.

It's easy enough to do, however, especially in a relationship that has lasted a while. You draw on a history of some trait or behavior your partner has exhibited in the past, and project it into the present and future. You cease to see the reality because you've let your negative expectations dim your view. Even when your partner changes, you don't see it or accept it.

You can choose to do better by your partner. Start by remembering that change is the one constant in life. As long as life continues, inevitable change can be channeled in a constructive direction. Keep in mind that living in a confined space can actually stunt a person's growth. It is the same with mental growth. By refusing your partner the room to grow, you may actually be limiting your partner. Your attitude shrinks your capacity to give and accept love.

When we resist the temptation to pigeonhole, we cultivate some of the most powerfully positive forces that exist. We exhibit faith in our partners' intrinsic goodness. We exercise hope in their potential for positive change. And we put love into meaningful action.

11.

Expect Surprises

Knowing another person intimately is surely one of the great joys of human relationships. But eventually, you may come to the point when you believe that you know all that there is to know. You interpret what you experience and observe in your partner through a single viewpoint. You become immune to surprises. Your expectations of sameness close your mind to the complexity of your partner, and you settle into stasis—relationship stagnation.

Understand that what you are experiencing is common. In essence, it is unfair to both you and your partner, but it doesn't make you the bad guy any more than your point of view makes your partner the boring, stagnant creature that you've imagined. It does, however, demand that you do some mental swimming if you want to get out of the muck.

To begin with, recognize the fact of your limited point of view, no matter how well you think that you know your partner. You've created a sort of shorthand understanding that saves a lot of soul-searching in response to your partner's traits and habits. But in the process, you may also have stopped seeing clearly.

A new view may seem hard to come by. Yet your partner has other acquaintances than you, and you have opportunities to absorb others' perceptions of her. The perspective of another person may be just the medicine you need to open your mind to the surprises still within your partner.

Time apart from your loved one can serve you well. When you return, allow yourself a quick moment to *really* observe, as though you don't know this person at all. Open your mind to subtle impressions that you often miss. Imagine that this is the first time you've met, and consider how you would see this person if you were forming a first impression.

Spending time together in the company of others can also be eye-opening. Put a roomful of people between you and your mate and observe from a distance. Pay attention to the person your mate is without you at her side. Stifle your expectations, and wait to be surprised.

Life is full of surprises—and so are people, if you take the time to look. Be curious and take a second look at your loved one. You don't know it all. Be thankful for that.

12.

Appreciate the Benefits
of a Doubt

Doubts hit hardest when we're tired or depressed, overcommitted or dealing with a crisis of some sort. Understanding this simple fact of human tendency may help offset the power of a doubt. And it may serve as a wakeup call to change the way we're living. But we still need to deal with the doubt itself.

The one response that does not seem to help is the "ignore it and it'll go away" approach. Ignoring your feelings gives them room to grow. But your doubts will surface again, and they will be magnified.

If you have doubts in your relationship, depending on what they are, you can use them as a catalyst to remember all of the wonderful things about your mate that make the doubts ridiculous. Doing this may even remind you to praise and give thanks to your partner. "Have I mentioned recently how much it means to me that you…?" In the context of such a conversation, you might even choose to reveal the doubt to your partner—which in turn can allow your mate to offer reassurances that put everything back in perspective.

On the other hand, doubts may actually serve as pointers to aspects of your relationship that need attention. You may suddenly realize how little you have been doing as a couple lately, or that you need to know more about your shared financial situation. Perhaps a doubt will awaken you to needs that your partner is feeling, or you may sense that it's time to rethink some habits the two of you have fallen into that are not in your shared best interests.

Your doubts will come and go. Instead of allowing them to rule you, use them constructively to eliminate some of life's more troubling stresses.

13.

Study the "Who's Who" of Living Together

Sharing a life with another person means weaving together two separate bodies, with two minds and two sets of choices, talents and potential. Ideally, a partnership serves both people and makes a whole greater than its parts. But differences can lead to intolerance and the desire to remake your partner to be like you. When you try to turn your mate into a mirror image of yourself, the fabric of the relationship begins to unravel.

As unlikely as it may sound, this intolerance sometimes stems from a loss of identity. In exaggerated form, psychologists refer to it as "enmeshment." We blur the lines between self and other. What our partners are and do becomes personally threatening to us when we don't approve of or appreciate it. We take our partners on as though they reflect on us or we are somehow responsible for them, as well.

Well, here's the good news. You are you. Your partner is another person. You can let your partner be different, even when you perceive the difference as something wrong. It does not make you less of the person you want to be.

The differences between you and your partner and the reactions that they provoke may challenge you to question many of the assumptions on which you base your daily choices. Perhaps you'll be confirmed in where you stand and what you are. Perhaps you'll discover new possibilities that allow you to create a new, more meaningful foundation. In either case, you'll have that person sitting across the kitchen table from you to thank for the revelations.

In addition, the differences between you and your partner require lessons in flexibility. There's a saying in the practice of yoga that has a compelling corollary in life: "Youth is a flexible spine." The human spirit that cannot touch its metaphorical toes is a calcified, unyielding spirit. The stretching exercises that come with tolerating differences bring new youth and vitality to your spirit. Instead of despising the differences you meet in your mate, cherish them for the texture that they provide.

14.

Find a Room of Your Own

It's a fact of human biology that the body needs time to repair and rebuild. That's what sleep is all about. We also take time to refuel throughout the day by eating and drinking. If we keep pushing ourselves without honoring these needs, we "hit the wall." Our physical needs take over and we are forced to stop.

Unfortunately, your psychological need for rest and repair is neither as obvious nor as insistent. You can go for long periods of time without tending to your emotional and spiritual needs, never diagnosing the malaise of spirit that results. You notice your short fuse, perhaps. You may sense that you aren't coping up to your normal standards. You blame circumstances, your partner, or others, when relief lies within, not without.

Loving relationships, meaningful activity, the knowledge that you have a place in your community, and plain old fun—these things make life rich and fulfilling. When you give yourself little or no quiet time alone for reflection and rest, however, you can quickly lose sight of what matters. You get caught up in commitments and being busy, and then one day, you wake up with a deep desire to stop the world and jump off. There are too many unending demands, and no time or place to repair has left you spent.

Imagine the psychological equivalent of a good meal at a leisurely pace. You make the time and create the setting. Then you nourish your mind and spirit by letting the dust settle and sorting out thoughts and feelings. Give yourself the pleasure of reading that book that you've wanted to pick up. Take a warm bath or get a massage. Take a long walk without the obligation to keep someone else's pace or carry on a conversation. Any form of refueling works, as long as it is something you choose entirely for yourself.

To take the time to serve your spirit is a gift to your partner, as well as yourself. To allow the same in kind only enhances what you have together. It may take some conversation to reassure that this move does not grow out of growing apart. But it pays dividends in renewed resources for coping and revitalizing your vision of what life can be.

15.

Lose the Laundry List

It is impossible for life partners not to develop some frustrations and disappointments with one another over time. Unfortunately, this material creates a growing laundry list of complaints. We take note of the negative, mentally and emotionally record it, and let it work on us and our responses to our mates.

The first step in losing the laundry list is to *acknowledge what you are feeling*. Once again, he forgot to add milk to the grocery list, and you have to make an emergency run to the store. She "cleaned up" your papers, even though you asked her not to, and now that receipt is nowhere to be found. Or that tired joke was made at your expense again while dining out with friends. You're angry or hurt or feeling disrespected. Admit what you're feeling to yourself, and you open the door to a positive approach to the negative feelings instead of letting them fester and grow.

Now, *forgive the person*. Your negative feelings may be entirely appropriate, or they may not. In either case, if you carry them around inside, you close yourself off to healing and build a wall between you and your partner. You may need to vent by saying something like, "When you do that, I feel…" Or you may choose not to speak. The essence of forgiveness has to do with releasing yourself from the negative feelings and exercising your capacity to love your partner beyond any weaknesses. Each of us has our own share of flaws. How would you wish your partner to respond to those traits and behaviors in you that are less than perfect?

Next, *forget the gripe.* Complaints are like bad dreams. If you move on after them, they lose their impact, but if you relive them again and again in your mind or conversation, they grow out of proportion to their real importance. Let them go. Holding on to your grievances will hurt you more than anyone else, and it will crowd out the possibility for positive change.

Now, *practice having a positive perspective.* Your partner almost certainly has shortcomings. So do you. But your partner also has strengths that deserve better than equal attention. As important, reconsider your judgment of some of your partner's "flaws." Often what we judge as negative in another is more a matter of simple differences. He may forget to add items to the grocery list because he's a dreamer, a creative type. The world needs dreamers and creators. She may clean up out of a desire to make a beautiful home for both of you. That's a wonderful impulse that deserves the compromises necessary to allow her to fulfill it.

In short, there is no end to gripes and grievances. But you can choose to lose the laundry list.

16.

Appreciate the Present

Worries about the future. Regrets about the past. These are the food of sleepless nights and anxious days. Many a present moment is squandered being troubled over either what's done and gone, or what may never happen.

Certainly, memories offer insight and allow us to relive happy times and recall the people that we love. Thoughts about the future can serve us well as we consider how to keep moving in the directions that we want. But when these thoughts turn to events and eventualities that we have no power to control or change, we waste the time we've been given instead of living and appreciating it. When you burden your mate with past troubles and future uncertainties, the experience of the moment is tainted.

Human nature and modern culture may conspire to push you in this direction, but you can choose to be present and live fully in each moment. Begin by noticing when your mood shifts in an irritable or anxious direction. Run a quick inventory of what you've had on your mind in the moments preceding this change. Were you thinking about a decision or event that you can do something about? If so, can you do something about it *now*? If not, you've sacrificed the present for some other time. Make a note to yourself about future action you can take, and then consciously put ruminations aside. Be where you are now.

In company, quietly focus on the others present. Make eye contact when they speak to you. Listen more than you speak. Remember to ask questions and pay attention to the answers you receive. Watch the way everyone interacts with each other, and take note of what you find especially appealing about each.

When you're doing something—whether it's washing the car, preparing a meal, or playing tennis—concentrate on one thing at a time. For the duration of that activity, push all competing activities and thoughts aside. They will all be there when you're through.

These exercises can help you recognize ways in which you typically miss the present. They help you learn to be in one place at a time and immerse yourself in your task. In reality, this moment is all that you have. Live it like you mean it.

17.

Expect to Learn

When you were younger, you moved through childhood like a little sponge, soaking up information and learning skills. You made messes and experimented. You were not surprised or dismayed by trial and error.

As you aged, the learning process slowed, in some cases to such an extent that your adulthood has come to have a static, fixed quality to it. You form firm opinions, max out certain skills, and define hard-and-fast limits of time and interest. You spend a lot of energy protecting yourself from potential pain and defending your point of view. In the process, you've lost curiosity about yourself, your partner, and perhaps your life, and you've shut down to learning new things.

When it comes to living life, your ability to think like a student plays a critical role. Life is an ongoing learning process. Your willingness to be a student of life can keep you from taking yourself too seriously. After all, you're not right all of the time. You still have much to learn. Accept the fifty-fifty probability that your partner can teach you something.

As a student, you must keep your perspective and keep trying when you don't "get it right." In adulthood, many of us suffer acute disappointment when we pursue something new and cannot immediately get it right. Too often we give up. When you see yourself as a student, you acknowledge that it could take years to learn, improve, and become "expert" at something. The fun resides in the journey to get there—even if you never actually arrive.

Being a student allows you to learn life's lessons. Frustrations can teach you patience, disagreements can become guides toward compassion and understanding, and disappointments can lead you to greater wisdom and perspective. These are proactive, optimistic responses to the ups and downs in life that *everyone* encounters.

Let yourself be a child again in the best sense of the word. This signifies a return to a dynamic view of life that relishes new ideas, skills, questions, and possibilities. It means forging ahead in the face of the learning curves, and worrying less about scraping your knees every once in a while.

18.

Speak Your Mind—
No One Will Read It

All people would like to believe that there is a partner out there for them who can read their mind. Unfortunately, mind-reading is a myth. And in intimate relationships, terrific stress is caused when one or both partners harbors such an expectation. If you want to be known and understood, you have to learn to speak your mind.

Not surprisingly, people often use the idea of self-expression as an excuse for poor communication styles. In the name of assertiveness, some people become bullies. Others latch on to otherwise sound methods of communicating with the primary goal of manipulating others into doing or giving what they want. Still others see the idea of speaking their minds as license to dump raw emotions on another human being. They vent their opinions, their aggressions, or their paranoia at the expense of others.

Practice communication that allows you to make yourself clear without raising your partner's defenses or impeding your partner's willingness to hear you out. It rarely serves to simply unload what's on your mind without thinking of how your words may be received. Consider how to speak so that your partner can listen without hearing a lot of static. Avoid the typical "hot" buttons that you've observed in the past. Frame your comments in ways so that they don't erupt as accusations. Leave criticism out of your communication, insofar as you're able. You're much more likely to be heard and understood this way than if you turn your communication into target practice.

Speak in terms of "I feel," "I believe," and "I think." As you speak, help your partner understand how you have arrived where you are and why you feel the need to express it. If what you are seeking to express is something you view as a problem, consider ahead of time some possible solutions that you can offer. Likewise, be willing to listen in return.

Many of the troubling issues we carry around in our heads—especially those relating to our significant others—become far larger than they should because we hold on to them too long without giving them voice. Speaking your mind offers you one more way to de-stress your lives together.

19.

Be the Bright Spot in
Your Partner's Day

Consider the typical scenario in a long-term relationship. Partners go their separate ways for the day's work. By the time the couple reunites, they've often spent the best part of their energy away from one another. The couple lands in the same place with two separate experiences logged, and the fun begins.

What happens next varies from couple to couple. You may not be ready at the moment of first contact with your partner to hear an outpouring of the day's woes and wows. Allow for decompression time—to change into different clothes, sit down with a cup of coffee, or take a short walk. Your partner's or your desire to take a breath before getting into the business of relating is not an insult. More likely, it's a psychological need that, if served, benefits both of you.

When you're ready and able to take time with one another, make sure that attention is given to each person. Perhaps one of you has the more compelling need to talk or the more interesting stories to tell, but both of you have had a day. Share and share alike. Nothing communicates love and sympathy better than taking an obvious interest in someone other than yourself.

If you're able to take time quietly sharing together, reunion time can be about working out details of your mutual life. Often, however, the end of a workday is not ideal. Tempers tend to be shorter. Every demand sounds bigger than it is. Consider carefully whether you are both in the right frame of mind to deal with what amounts to more work. If not, simply ask: "When would be a good time to talk this through?" Save demands and negotiations for moments of higher energy.

Oddly, good news from your partner's day is sometimes harder to handle than bad. You've had a bad day, and maybe you're a little blue. Your partner marches in with a beaming smile and announces a raise, a problem solved, or a great idea. Don't rain on your partner's parade. Good news can be scarce enough without having it dashed by a lousy mood. Muster the enthusiasm to smile, and make congratulations the order of the day.

Individuals are different from one another, and so are couples. Supporting one another in your separate responsibilities and efforts calls for attention and creativity. Only you know what works for you. Establish routines for time together that allow each of you to be the bright spot in your partner's day.

20.

Know Your Limits

One of modern society's most common woes is overload. People have more belongings and activities, have more information available, and engage in more multitasking than ever before. Overload does damage to our ability to cope, relate to others, and enjoy small moments. It inhibits concentration and causes a variety of stress-related ailments. Our culture does little to help us manage the load. The reality is that it's up to you to do something about it. But you may not have taken the time to learn your limits and design your life appropriately.

Your intimate relationship plays a vital role in this. Many of your choices are either mutual or interdependent, and the issue of overload bears working on together. Assess what you hope for together. What direction do you want your shared life to take? Where are you in relation to what you hope for? How do the elements that crowd your life serve or not serve that?

On a more immediate level, consider your own limits. Are you having more than your average number of accidents or mishaps? Does your mind wander? Is your primary relationship having more than its share of unexplained misfires? When was the last time you said no to an outside commitment? How often do you consider what you could easily take off your to-do list? What have you done lately to feed your spirit or enrich your intimate relationship?

Knowing your limits may very well be a lifelong project, but it won't happen unless you give it your attention. You may have to experiment. You may have to take sabbaticals from one or many commitments until you find a comfort zone in which you can gauge what's worth keeping and what has to go.

21.

Have an Adventure Together

Most of the time in a couple's busy life, it's easiest to do what's easy. If you find a restaurant that you like, you keep going back. If you pick a vacation spot that leaves you with great memories, you return there. If you find an activity that you both enjoy together, you make it a habit. You develop rituals and routines that relieve you of the need to be creative, and you settle into a comfortable pattern.

This way of managing your shared time has its benefits. It affords you predictable, consistent time together. It maintains a venue for communication and relaxation. It creates a sense of security. However, the comfort level can also backfire. You can fall into a state of complacency that blinds you to an increasing lack of vitality and mutual growth. While your habits are growing more similar, your souls are parting ways. Your conversations become perfunctory or circular without fresh ideas or new experiences to feed them.

It may be time for you and your partner to have some new adventures. An adventure can be as elemental as changing where you go for a walk or trying a new restaurant. It can take the form of local exploration. It may mean riding the train instead of driving, choosing a package tour over the family vacation spot, or foregoing the classical concert in favor of a jazz bar.

With new experiences come new revelations about one another. You may see a side of your partner that you've never seen before. External changes demand internal changes and growth. The adventures that you share will call on your resources, hone skills, and exercise your willingness and ability to cooperate. You will change, and you'll be doing it together.

You don't have to give up all of your routines and habits. Neither do you have to abandon old friends and venues that give you pleasure and a sense of continuity. Simply season what you have already established with the fresh spice of challenge, excitement, and adventure.

22.

Give When It's Least Expected

In our society, the card and gift industries have come largely to dictate when, what, and how we give for special occasions. That's not all bad. Plenty of us appreciate a remembrance for one reason or another, such as a birthday. But one of the peculiar effects of institutionalizing giving is the sense of obligation that has grown up around it. People come to expect certain gifts, particularly from their partners. They may feel hurt if they don't get them, or take it for granted when they do. If you're the giver, it's one more item on the to-do list, and in some cases, people may even resent the necessity.

And yet, isn't giving one of life's most pleasurable and rewarding ways of relating to our loved ones? Surely we don't want to suspend the practice of giving at times specifically designated to making our mates feel special. Nor do we want to let the commercialization of giving dictate how and when—or even if— we give to the people we love.

If giving has lost its meaning for you, rethink your habits. For starters, give more time and thought to what you're doing and why.

Perhaps you resent the fact that the greeting card industry dictates your giving. So choose an occasion that no one but you and your partner would understand as significant to give the most meaningful gift of the year. Or show up with a favorite bottle of wine just because it's Friday and you're grateful to share it with the most important person in your life. Take note when your partner is down or stressed, and let that be excuse enough to offer up your love in some tangible way.

Think about substituting time and effort for a purchased item. Wrap up a box with a promise inside. "Gift Certificate: for the redecoration of your study." "Let's make a night of it—your pick of place, time, and event." "IOU seven hours of baby-sitting—no strings attached—while you do what you want." Pick any item off the shared to-do list that your partner has waited a long time to see accomplished and do it just to express your love.

It's not what we do that matters most. It's how we do it and why. Make your giving meaningful. Give when it's least expected. Give from your heart.

23.

Turn Differences
into Complements

When you take the brave step of setting up housekeeping with your mate, you discover that all sorts of variations exist in terms of tastes, talents, styles, and preferences. Before long, you may find that you develop an adversarial relationship around the subject of how you differ, and your tempers flare. It's a shame to let this happen. Identify differences that seem to get in your way as a couple, and then stop and do some brainstorming before they grow into a pattern. Don't stop talking when you've identified the offensive behaviors or attitudes. Figure out how a behavior results in causing trouble between you.

For instance, suppose you appreciate being able to leave your wet shoes and umbrella on the porch as you come in from the rain. Your partner, however, feels that the porch makes a first impression on visitors and wants everything that isn't decorative kept out of sight. What's at stake? For your partner, an attractive, welcoming home. For you, convenience that helps you keep your property clean and orderly. What's the solution? Find ways to put each of your preferences to use. Create storage for your items on the porch that is attractive and convenient. You achieve a common goal, and both of you are happy.

Trade off responsibilities so that you both can fulfill your potential. For example, when you share the housecleaning, perhaps you are a meticulous duster. On the other hand, suppose your partner is great when the windows need washing. Divide the jobs so that each of you does what you do best. If you recognize the compensating strengths in your partner's style, you'll have an easier time tolerating what you perceive to be weaknesses.

Do you prefer different foods? Serve a greater variety of dishes, all in smaller portions, and make sure each of your preferences is honored. Do you tend toward different decorating styles? Designate rooms for each to have the final say, or learn to put different styles together for a more blended look. These examples may not touch your areas of difference, but they illustrate a spirit of compromise and respect.

24.

Lengthen Your Fuse

We all deal with circumstances that make us angry from time to time. Some people naturally take longer to lose their cool. Others seem to have been born with a ready temper. The fact is that we all have regular excuses for anger, and typical ways of dealing with it. For the record, a short fuse doesn't help anyone.

Your "fuse" might be defined as the amount of tolerance you have, measured in time and intensity, before you blow up in anger when provoked. If your fuse is short, you tend to react quickly. A short fuse will often short-circuit constructive communication with your partner, leading to unnecessary misunderstandings and pain. If your fuse tends to burn fast and furious, it is up to you to learn how to manage your temper more effectively.

Count to ten. When you force yourself to pause before you react, you allow your internal stress levels to settle. You may have to wait ten minutes, or even a day or two. As the initial flush recedes, you'll have the opportunity to regain some of your balance and perspective, and you can respond rationally.

Once you've simmered down, make an effort to stick to the issue at hand. We often make disagreements larger by loading them up with more than the present problem. Deal with one thing at a time. That tends to make problems far more manageable, and it's definitely fairer to whomever you're dealing with.

When responding to the source of anger, listen at least as much as you talk. Many of the aggravations that touch your life are not as clear-cut or one-sided as your anger tempts you to believe. As you fill in more of the details, you may find that your reaction was genuinely too dramatic. Rather than having to eat crow later, why not get all the facts first?

Finally, have some heart for the person who is either the object of or witness to your temper. How would you feel if you were on the receiving end? Most of us want fair treatment, the right to explain ourselves and our opinions, and the benefit of the doubt. Even on the sidelines, we would prefer at least a show of courtesy. It's not necessarily a cure-all to treat others the way you'd like to be treated, but it almost always moves you in a positive direction.

25.

Love with an Open Hand

When you try to hold someone's love by clinging and clutching, anything and everything out of your control threatens you and feeds your fears of loss and rejection. In many cases, clingy behavior is just as painful to your partner as it is to you, and it may actually drive your partner away.

Loving with an open hand requires you to take a leap of faith. It's important to understand that love that clings and clutches grows out of an essential lack of trust in your partner. Whether you know it or not, you are saying, "I don't think I can rely on your love." Now, you may be right. Perhaps your partner is not reliable or worthy of your trust. You can be sure of one thing, however. No one ever learned how to love faithfully by application of a stranglehold. When you enter into a relationship, at some level, you must decide to trust the other person. There's no way around it. Clinging doesn't work.

In the worst case, when you love with an open hand, you gain invaluable, if disappointing, knowledge about the person you love.

You gain the ability to make an informed decision about a future with this person. More likely, you'll experience the great joy of receiving love from another that is freely given. You'll gain confidence in your own worth and awareness of your independence. You'll also gain freedom from the doubts and fears that often plague couples.

The more you practice openhanded love, the more you reap the pleasures of letting go of that which you cannot control. An open hand is a hand prepared both to give and receive the best that life offers.

26.

Cherish the Child
in Your Partner

No matter how old we are, we all carry a child within—someone with curiosity and fears who longs to be cared for and protected. That part of us can surface during inopportune times and make us demanding, petty, and less mature.

On the other hand, that young soul within us generates some of our most delightful and spontaneous impulses. We forget to be guarded and enjoy a moment of free expression or simple, unmitigated joy. We believe in possibilities and still feel curious about life, others, and ourselves. That part of you may be buried under layers of caution or pain. Allowing your child within to blossom can be a great step in building a life that includes joy and hope.

You may not always recognize when your partner's childish needs are at the root of stress between you. In fact, your mate may not realize the impulses at work that stir up trouble. But if you understand that everyone needs to be nurtured—even adults—you can make taking care of each other a priority.

Nurturing means providing a shoulder to cry on. You need to allow your partner to show weakness. You may have to temporarily lay aside your impulse to fix things in order to offer support. You also may have to deal with your own vulnerabilities. If you want a partner who is the "strong" one all of the time, then nurturing may be more difficult for you. When you learn to sympathize with a comforting embrace, you give your partner the chance to feel emotion honestly.

Nurturing also involves encouragement. You may be the one who needs to encourage your partner to rise to a challenge. Whether it's taking a new job, learning a new skill, or simply having an adventure, your partner may face such a challenge with the same mix of excitement, longing, and fear that a child experiences when learning such things as how to ride a bike. You can be the one who says, "Go for it!" or "I know you can do it." Nurturing means that no matter what the outcome is, you're still there, ready to encourage again.

27.

Try on a Different Pair of Shoes

One of the great joys of intimacy is the close connection that allows you to know another human being almost as well as you know yourself. A key ingredient to building that kind of knowledge is recognizing that your mate is much more than half of your couple. Your partner also continues to be an individual, no matter how close you become. This can be threatening—we all suffer fears related to what we don't know. But it can also be invigorating and exciting if you take the time and effort to step into your partner's shoes from time to time.

When you're mystified by your mate's reaction to something, seek to understand. You may feel that in most situations, you can predict how your mate will respond. It's when your partner surprises you that you have an opportunity to learn more.

Seek to get a clear picture of your partner's viewpoint. You won't see through his eyes if you're plotting your strategy or framing your response the entire time that he is explaining. You may discover that he has thought of things you haven't, or has a creative notion worthy of considering. After your partner has shared his perspective, take some time before you respond in order to let it really soak in, and allow the possibility that you may change your mind as a result.

When your mate is upset, open the door to a conversation about the source of his agitation. This means choosing to be a listener rather than a judge or adviser, asking questions, and quietly waiting for the answers instead of offering analysis or solutions. You'll never reach a true understanding of how your partner feels and why unless you suspend your input long enough for him to tell you. And your partner is far more likely to make a habit of telling you his problems if you become a good listener.

28.

Live the Life That You
Always Hoped to Have

Often people write off much more than they should as impossible to affect or change. Perhaps they neglect to take the initiative when an opportunity arises. Or they accept someone else's evaluation of them without question or objection, even when at some level, they believe that other person may be wrong. Maybe they stop paying attention and miss the moments when they might move in a direction that would improve the life they're leading. Too frequently in any of these situations, people hold their mates responsible for what only they can change.

The only way to move beyond such a state is to admit the fact that positive change and growth come primarily not from outside yourself, but from within. How you face the hand that has been dealt to you and how you choose to play it make all the difference.

If you don't regularly examine your life, start now. Are you moving in the direction that you want? Do you sense a void that needs to be filled? Take stock, and do it often.

Building self-awareness gives you a foundation. But knowing what and how to build is also important. Allow yourself to dream. Your best plans will grow out of your passions—the people and pursuits that light a fire within you.

As you dream and identify aspects of the life that you really want to live, you have a better basis for making positive changes. For example, perhaps some further education is in order in your life, but you've been deferring your own plans while tending to the needs of others. Some creative thinking and plotting may allow you to find compromises that let you make some steps of your own, even while you're supporting others.

If you're frustrated with your life on a fundamental level, small problems are going to have disproportionate power to bother you. Alternatively, if you're making headway, however slowly, in a direction that excites you, the life you want will unfold before you.

29.

Build Bridges Instead of Walls

Walls go up when conflict occurs, and conflict happens in any close relationship. However conflict arises, it tends to call up your instinct for self-protection. You don't like to feel attacked, rejected, or dismissed. You separate yourself from the aftermath—that residual coolness, suspicion, or irritability that lingers in the relationship.

Aggression is classic building material for a wall of defense. Your partner refuses to respond when you air a complaint or an issue, so you attack in the name of making your point. Or your partner is the one launching the attack, and you put up your dukes to give as good as you get.

You may choose a wall of different material. Perhaps you meet accusations or criticisms with rationalization. The more you defend your position, the less open you become to your partner's point of view. The wall between the two of you builds. Walls also go up when you choose to ignore controversies that arise between you.

Regardless of the way in which you build a wall, you put a barrier in the way of communication and understanding, and you impede the process of resolution.

Walls grow up in the empty space created when you and your partner pull apart. Conflict serves as the stick of dynamite that opens a gaping hole between the two of you. That space will be filled in one way or another. A more hopeful choice is a bridge. Unlike a wall, a bridge connects your two sides.

When you choose to hear out your partner in the midst of argument, you choose to start a bridge to her. Give her time to express thoroughly the perspective she brings to the conflict. Listen carefully, but also ask for clarification. Step out of your own concerns long enough to genuinely seek to understand her viewpoint.

A bridge depends on communicating your own point of view, too. The conflict develops in the first place because people with differing opinions are butting heads. Unless both of you have a hearing, you will have a hard time meeting somewhere in the middle.

The connection you create when you build a bridge to your mate comes from letting the conflict end. It's hard to let a disagreement go. You keep coming back to your point. You want your partner to say you're right. It's best to come to terms. Compromise and agree to disagree. Then let it go, and move on.

30.

Emphasize the Estimable

The reactions you have to your partner's character and choices have an enormous impact on his self-esteem. If your mate feels judged and found wanting day after day, he will respond with an increasingly defensive stance. He will begin to retreat, feeling badly about himself and angry toward you. By focusing on the negative, you're actually feeding it and helping it grow. However, it's possible to deal more productively with your partner's mistakes and weaknesses. If you face the difficulties and seek positive solutions, you become a real partner—an ally—who can be depended on "for better or worse."

First, test your own perceptions. You may, out of frustration, be elevating a harmless difference to the level of character flaw. Do some soul-searching before you get carried away with your partner's problems. In that context, it's good to admit your own shortcomings, if only to yourself. None of us is perfect, and that includes you. As hard as it may be sometimes, it doesn't hurt to admit your weaknesses to your partner, as well. Doing so reinforces the fact that however much you criticize your partner, you understand that you can justifiably be criticized in return.

More importantly, make sure that you notice the positive in your partner, as well as the negative, and give it equal or more of your attention. Think about what you admire in your partner, and let your loved one know. The aspects that trouble you will seem far less important when you remember what is estimable.

Continue to voice your essential confidence in your mate. There's little that's more inspiring than a steady diet of "I believe in you." When problems arise, such a message reinforces a solution-oriented approach. Instead of communicating, "I can't believe you could do something this awful," you say, "I know you're capable of much better." It will remind you that the problems don't define your mate.

The habit of emphasizing the estimable creates an atmosphere of positive reinforcement. It feeds those aspects of your mate and your relationship that you *want* to grow. There are times when your complaints have to be aired, and problems have to be faced and solved. But if those times occur in a typically supportive, respectful environment, your mistakes won't drive you apart. They will become your bridge to success.

31.

Fly in Formation

When we choose to ignore the demands of partnership in favor of our own preferences, we set the scene for unnecessary conflict and competition. Instead of doing the work needed to make mutual decisions and find solutions that both partners can live with, we create adversarial situations that raise the stakes. Stress levels rise and the relationship becomes a battleground. You may get your way, but the price is almost certainly too dear.

Your first choice ought to be to cooperate. In contests of this sort, you can find a common interest under all the layers of conflict. If you choose to sit down and seek a compromise that is acceptable to your partner, a small matter could be put in its place and strengthen the bond between you.

Nature illustrates this beautifully. Canadian geese migrate thousands of miles every year. Most of us have seen them tracing a V-shape against an autumn sky. There's more to what we see, though. The wind foil created by the birds in the forward tip of the

V-formation actually makes the flying easier for birds in their wake. While some of the birds do the heavy lifting, the others rest. Furthermore, when the lead bird tires, it falls back to the end of the formation while another, more rested bird takes its place. It is a ballet of cooperation and support that strengthens the flock's potential to survive and thrive.

Humans don't seem to have an instinctual response to shared interests. We often choose conflict over cooperation. We must choose to find the will to work together. What we don't know by instinct, we can learn by example and experiment. You and your partner can fly in formation when you decide to do it.

32.

Choose Where You Are

We all view our lives through lenses, and our different perceptions serve as the filters. No filter seems to be more limiting than the belief that you are trapped. You see yourself as stuck—in your relationship, in your circumstances, in your job, or in your physical condition. This attitude steals your motivation and your courage.

Admittedly, there are circumstances and relationships that are not what you would hope. You may unexpectedly have a disabled mate to care for. You may reach the glass ceiling in the job that you're trained to do, and see nowhere to go. Your family circumstances may have used up all of your resources and prevented you from getting ahead of the expense curve. In such cases, it's tempting to say, "This can't or won't change. I'm trapped."

This attitude is born of feelings, not facts. The partner whose mate suffers unfixable disability has a choice to either remain in the relationship or not. The person whose job possibilities have dried up can choose to stay put, to quit and live the life of a drifter, or to start again on a new career track. The family living on the financial edge chooses whether to struggle, or to reconsider lifestyle choices that prevent their money from stretching. Some of these choices may sound far-fetched, but there are people choosing each of them every day.

The point is that the choices you make are your life. You stay in a relationship with someone whose health is gone most likely out of love, and the conviction that it's the right thing to do. When you recognize the fact that you've made that choice, your vantage point changes. You are no longer trapped in an impossible situation. Instead, you are living by your principles and taking a courageous, loving path. You could choose differently. When you finally acknowledge responsibility for where you are, whom you are with, and what you are doing, you open the trap.

Living with choice requires that you consider the whys and wherefores of what you've decided so far. Have you made choices that you can continue to stand behind? What do you believe to be important? How do you move forward? These are big questions. Your answers offer perspective that can change your view of your life and your experience of it, as well.

33.

Forget to Keep Score

Love can bear a striking resemblance to a contest sometimes. The contest may start out in good fun, but played out over time and in conjunction with the ordinary annoyances and frustrations of daily life, the contest can become a more serious tug of war. The resolution comes when someone finally declares, "You owe me one!"

Granted, it's usually good to put an issue to rest. And sometimes compromise calls for taking turns getting your own way. But if this style of negotiation becomes the mindset, partners will find themselves on opposing sides.

The give-and-take of an intimate relationship doesn't have to follow this path. It requires something more to serve one another's needs with as much enthusiasm as you serve your own. In particular, it rests on a true appreciation of what it means to be a team.

An effective team accommodates the ups and downs of each team member. In a partnership, this means that when one person is vulnerable, tired, or stressed, the other picks up the slack. When one member is full of energy and imagination, the other supports those talents and creativity. Every "point" scored is another for the team, not for one member or the other.

In practical terms, this means first taking regular time to build your sense of teamwork. Daily rituals of mealtimes or even phone calls can be used to reinforce your commitment to one another. Regular dates, when the rest of the world is temporarily excluded (including your kids), can provide much-needed privacy to give one another support. Periodic times when you sit down and go over the practical matters of your partnership—finances, plans, mutual worries, and shared pleasures—can keep you on the same wavelength and build the solid rapport that any team needs to do its best.

Most of all, consciously play to your partner's strengths. It's okay to acknowledge that you've got a streak of selfishness in the mix. Just put it to work for your relationship by recognizing that you serve your own interests when you give your mate ample opportunities to shine—to "win." If there's any score to keep in your relationship, it's the tally of all the ways you're bringing out the best in one another and building a winning team.

34.

Make the First Move

"Stalemate" is the term for what happens when two partners insist that it isn't their responsibility to fix a problem. Each person becomes unwilling to change, bend, or even initiate a conversation. What sits too long in one place indeed turns stale.

Here's another good term: "deadlock." This defines the head-butting of two equal forces, leading to horns locked together. The "dead" part of the word raises the specter of two great animals slowly dying because they've locked themselves into a bind that makes it impossible for them to reach food or water.

It's amazing how often people get caught up in their own convictions. They become convinced that they hold the moral high ground and refuse to be the one who breaks free from the controversy. To do any less—that is, to initiate a solution—is to show a weakness.

So for reasons of character and effectiveness, why shouldn't you make the first move? Breaking a stalemate requires humility. You'll never move forward unless you can honestly say, "I may not have the whole story," or "I may be wrong." Even if you don't see *how* you may be wrong, simply acknowledging the possibility can have a softening effect on another person.

Breaking a stalemate also requires empathy. Your partner has reasons, just as you do, for being stubborn. Put yourself in your mate's shoes and consider how painful your inflexible attitude may feel to her. Take some time to imagine why your partner's point of view makes sense to her. Until you can honestly conceive of another way of seeing whatever it is you're battling over, you won't be able to approach reconciliation with integrity.

Most of all, breaking a stalemate requires leadership. You take the initiative. You develop a plan and make the move. Perhaps you feel that doing so means sacrificing your own best interests. The truth is actually the opposite: When you choose to be the leader—to show by example that you wish to avoid deadlock—you achieve your own freedom. Your partner may choose to stand still, regardless. In that case, it becomes her problem. You have released yourself to move on.

More often than not, if you're willing to move and soften your position in some way, your partner will move, as well. Frame your forward motion in terms of your love for one another and your future together, and you may find that the source of your trouble doesn't look quite so important or immutable.

35.

Learn to Breathe

Autonomic responses—the involuntary activities of your heart, lungs, nervous system, and glands—are often the first to exhibit the effects of stress. Learning to be aware of these can help you recognize when your stress levels are especially high. Your heart rate increases, you break out in a sweat, and your adrenaline kicks into overdrive. You may suffer an outbreak of acne, notice that your hair has lost its luster, or have trouble concentrating. And you may overreact more readily to issues with your mate.

After self-awareness comes the opportunity to change your natural responses to stress. Chief among the positive changes you can make is learning to physically relax. Relaxation can lower blood pressure, balance production of hormones, and stimulate your body's release of endorphins—proteins in your system that act to offset pain. If stress is a big factor in your life, finding literature and courses on relaxation may be in order. But even for those who have only the average number of stress-producers in their lives, some simple relaxation practices can help prevent you from being taken over by pressures of the moment.

First, learn to breathe. *How* you breathe can have a profound effect on your ability to think, relax, and maintain some overall physiological balance. The most beneficial breathing uses full lung capacity and occurs slowly. Such breathing improves the condition and circulation of your blood, relieves both mental and physical fatigue, and aids your body in its natural processes of repair and revitalization.

Sit in a quiet place. Concentrate solely on breathing, inhaling very slowly through your nose and pushing out your abdomen at the same time. This has the effect of pulling down on your diaphragm, which in turn pulls the breath you inhale into your lower lungs. Continue to breathe in, paying attention to how your stomach and chest rise as air fills your lungs. When your chest is fully expanded, hold your breath for a slow count of five. Then begin to breathe out slowly through your nose, letting your chest collapse first, followed by your stomach, and finally your abdomen. Repeat this exercise five times.

In moments of high stress, breathing in this manner offsets your natural tendency to tense up. If you make this breathing technique a regular habit—say, for five to ten minutes, once a day—you will gain a new appreciation of how different a relaxed state feels from a tense one.

36.

Think with Your Heart,
Feel with Your Head

Most couples experience some degree of misunderstanding in their day-to-day lives together. While an in-depth analysis of the misunderstandings might be instrumental in alleviating them, even simply acknowledging that you don't always understand what you receive from one another can help. You can slow down and maintain a sense of proportion about your disagreement, and it can motivate you to seek better ways to understand the person closest to you.

We receive information from many sources and in a lot of different ways. This information becomes building material for what we consider knowledge, and on a good day, wisdom. We move most successfully from facts to insights when we allow our reason and emotions—head and heart—to work together. Sometimes, however, either head or heart takes over. That's when we find little misunderstandings blossoming into full-blown conflicts.

Consider what happens when an off-handed remark from your partner hits you the wrong way. You feel hurt, angry, or shaken. The emotion has the potential to become so prominent that it diminishes your ability to reason. Your heart is in overdrive while your head idles. Yet this is precisely the moment when you need to use your head—to consciously put your most realistic, constructive, positive thoughts in gear. Before you attack your partner based on complete emotion, admit the probability that your mate has and will screw up, because that's human. Remember the important parts of your partner's worthy character and best intentions. When your head talks to your heart like this, you will be able to clarify what was meant in what your partner said. Then you will you be able to let the hurt go.

On the other hand, perhaps when confronted with confusion or conflict, you lead with your head. Thoughts, like feelings, have a way of picking up momentum that can quickly escalate misunderstandings. You may find yourself stuck on a merry-go-round of doubts and fears and seek to feel better by lashing out. Or perhaps you rush to judgment and cease to listen because you've already found your partner guilty as charged.

Now start using your heart. The minute your mind starts turning down those dark corridors of doubt, judgment, and negativity, you need to draw on your reserves of love, and let emotion transform your thinking. Marry your heart to your mind so that your thoughts are better informed. You'll get beyond the misunderstanding instead of feeding it.

37.

Aim for the Extraordinary

For some reason, after the extraordinary events of falling in love and making commitments, some people settle for an ordinary life together. Perhaps it's what they've been taught to expect by the examples of their parents and others. Maybe it's evidence of a lack of energy or imagination. Whatever the reason, after having "arrived" in a relationship, some people aim for nothing more wonderful than the ordinary, and that's just what they get.

Why settle? Why not aim to be unusual, extraordinary, and remarkable—unusually attached to one another, extraordinarily alive in the moment, and remarkably in touch with what's happening between and around you? Imagine if your friends and neighbors could say, "I've never known a couple that treats each other with such respect," or "I envy the wonderful friendship that they have."

Obviously, no one can define what you find desirable and extraordinary in your unique relationship. Only you and your mate know what matters most to the two of you. Maybe your sweetest dream is world travel. Have you incorporated that into your daily decisions together? If a life that includes exotic destinations falls within your definition of extraordinary, are you aiming for it?

Making something extraordinary of your partnership may begin with the vision and determination of only one of you. You may have to do the lion's share of motivating. Happily, most people harbor a secret desire to have a special life with a special person. If you take steps to imagine and promote a relationship that rises above the ho-hum, your partner will catch your vision.

But it takes two to create a solid picture of what you're actually aiming to be and do together. Beyond agreeing that you want an extraordinary life as a pair, give yourselves time to fantasize together. The changes that people are able to actualize, once they identify what they want, are amazing. Couples have left high-salary jobs in the corporate world to open small local businesses that they can operate and build on together. People have moved from lifelong familiar locations to settle in a climate or terrain for which they have discovered a particular affinity. Others have chosen to make themselves active volunteers in charities, hands-on relief work abroad, or hospital programs.

So many possibilities exist that it would take a library to explore half of them. The best research is the research you and your partner do yourselves, starting with discovering which dreams about which opportunities in life touch you most meaningfully and passionately. Aim for something better than an ordinary life, and you're likely to find it.

38.

Extend Your Reach

It's easy to ignore our subtle mental and physical losses that happen over time. They usually occur so slowly that we don't notice them, until we suddenly discover that what used to come easily has become seriously challenging to us. Such losses occur when we cease to challenge various aspects of ourselves. Atrophy sets in, and with it a low-level discontent that focuses on the smallest of annoyances and disappointments within us.

This is where a disciplined learning curve comes into play. Certainly, there may be reasons for changes in your capacity of body and mind. Illness and injury can do irreparable damage sometimes. Youth is inevitably replaced with middle and old age, if you're fortunate to live that many years. But your spirit will shrink only if you capitulate to inertia and cease to look for high ground.

When was the last time you sought out an opinion that challenged one of your own set views? Listening to alternative voices—through reading, attending lectures, or involving yourself with a variety of people—stretches your preconceptions. It encourages you to rethink your own assumptions and consider other possibilities.

How often do you try to do something you've never done before? Maybe it shouldn't be downhill skiing, but what about joining a charity-sponsored walkathon? Or taking part in the community holiday concert? Or attending a gourmet cooking class? Simply taking the initiative to involve yourself in something new can increase your circle of acquaintances.

When do you make room for people of different generations and backgrounds from your own? Do you go places and attend events that include young people and children? When you step outside of familiar territory, do you stretch and grow to accommodate new experiences, people, and information?

Reaching beyond your set limits stretches your spirit and builds your self-respect. You can continue to challenge yourself and develop your character until the end of your days. With a mind kept limber by reaching for new ideas and a spirit kept buoyant by interest in other people, you will continue to gain perspective, wisdom, and inner agility.

39.

Know Who You Are

When we attend school as children and young adults, we understand that education is a body of facts that we need to know before we reach maturity. As high school ends, however, a subtle shift occurs. There's no lack of factual material still available to learn, of course, and depending on the direction we take, we may have many miles to travel through academic and technical programs of learning. But as time goes by, we discover another learning curve upon which all others will eventually need to be built if we want to live a life that is meaningful.

For some, the awakening occurs when it's time to choose a major in college, a job out of school, or a person to share a serious relationship. A bewildering number of possibilities exist, and sometimes they don't see any options that stand out from the rest. They take the "eeny, meeny, miney, moe" approach, or bow to the pressure of mentors or peers. The basic issue is often not how well they're getting the external facts and skills under their belts. It's what they know or don't know about themselves.

Knowing ourselves gives us a strong foundation on which to build all aspects of a life well-lived. But we have to pursue it. We have to make ourselves the subjects of our own scrutiny and appraisal. We need to accept the hard lessons and be receptive to the unexpected.

Give yourself time to get to know yourself. You need quiet moments that are set aside for reflection and introspection. It's virtually impossible to understand yourself better in light of your experiences and emotional responses if you never give them any later thought.

Let pain be one of your teachers. Psychological pain in the face of loss, failure, embarrassment, and fear have the potential to pull you up short. Pain can offer invaluable lessons about how you tick, what and whom you care about, and why some aspects of your life are not working. It also may reveal the gap between what and who you *wish* you were, and the reality.

Let passion guide you. The events, places, and people that set you alight have something to teach. It is in these that you'll discover your unique gifts and interests. When you follow your heart, you'll find yourself in the process, and the rest will begin to fall into place.

40.

Be a Cheerleader
Instead of a Critic

When it comes to criticism, no one can cut as close to the bone as the one who knows you most intimately. Over a time of experiencing criticism, you can end up feeling pretty lonely and unappreciated, and you may lose your confidence. You may become your own harshest critic. Plainly, this scenario doesn't make for a happy relationship.

No one can rival you if you choose to be your mate's most avid fan. In the same way that you are privy to your partner's weaknesses, you have an inside view of the good. Knowing all that you know, choose to emphasize the good, and the message will be powerful, indeed.

Be honest in your cheering, and offer your encouragement free of charge. If you're angling for something in return, it will rob what you have to say of its credibility and helpfulness. Most important of all, offer your cheers in the context of love. If you offer words of support despite the possibility of a disappointing outcome, you communicate volumes about your respect, trust, and maturity. In effect, you say, "Go ahead and try your best. The worst that can happen is that you won't succeed, and that's okay, too."

Be critical of another person long enough and you may find that person living up to your most negative forecasts. Make an effort instead to notice the best qualities of that person, and you and your partner may soon be mining the gold together. You will be a safe, sheltering presence in your partner's universe, the presence we all need in a world with too many critics.

41.

Assume Nothing but the Best

Making assumptions about people's actions can have a profound effect on the way that you receive and respond to information. The very same circumstance can fill you with joy or foreboding, depending on what you assume about it.

Suppose, for example, that your mate arrives home one evening with a beautiful bouquet of flowers. Maybe the two of you have had a lot of pressures with one another of late. You may be wary about your mate's motivations. Is he feeling guilty about something? Does he think you'll just forget about what was said the other night? You assume the negative, robbing the giver of a gesture that may very well be genuine, and the beauty of the flowers is lost on you.

In truth, no matter how suspicious your thoughts may be about the intentions of your mate, unless you have it directly from him or have irrefutable evidence, *you really cannot know* what's going on inside that other person. You do no good by assuming his motivations are negative. If you have to assume anything, make it the best until proven otherwise.

You could have past experiences that color your point of view and make it hard to assume the best. In this case, choose to wait and see; to assume nothing at all. If your partner offers an explanation that you doubt, wait a while. If you've been told the truth, other details will surface that corroborate your partner's sincerity and honesty. If your partner has been less than candid, that, too, will come out.

You add many hours of negative feelings to your primary relationship when you make assumptions. Life is too short to make a big deal about what you *don't* know. If you are determined to assume—what something signifies, what happens when you're not around, or what another person is thinking—assume the best. If, on the other hand, you prefer to base your actions, thoughts, and plans on what is right in front of you, then discipline your imagination and forego the assumptions altogether. Make an effort to discover the truth, or let the truth come out in its own good time. In so doing, you will increase the peace in your life and offer the maximum dignity to your partner's.

42.

Create an Atmosphere
of Tolerance

Rapid transportation, instant communication, and a growing amount of cross-fertilization in the media, arts, and entertainment have added an amazing amount of diversity into our day-to-day lives. The net effect is a growing appreciation for the fact that people come in all sizes, shapes, colors, and cultures. Tolerance has become a hallmark of civilized societies.

Perhaps it isn't altogether surprising, however, that the positive lessons about tolerance sometimes stop at our own front doors. But the same ideas do apply. There are differences between partners that have to do with opinions, personalities, strengths, habits, gender, religion, background, family, and education. Such differences require that you and your partner create and maintain an atmosphere of tolerance between you.

"Tolerance" means that you appreciate what is meaningful to your partner, even when you cannot understand it. Perhaps you were raised in a family that moved regularly from place to place. You may become restless if you stay in one location for very long. But if your mate spent her entire life in her hometown, an urge to move may be unappealing to her. However you negotiate such a difference, begin by appreciating the diversity of your experiences and desires. Imagine putting down roots and playing bridge once a week with a friend from kindergarten! On the other hand, imagine starting fresh with new people and possibilities every few years.

Tolerance also means that you accept your partner's beliefs, even if you do not subscribe to them. People's convictions make sense to them. Part of respecting your partner is respecting those convictions. Perhaps over time, you may develop beliefs you have in common. But you can be sure that they won't develop out of a spirit of animosity or proselytizing. They will grow in the context of love and acceptance.

If you haven't grown up in the same culture, you may find certain aspects of your mate's family practices annoying or intrusive. Yet if these practices have importance to her, you do her an injustice to insist that your preferences must rule. Find ways to compromise or meld different backgrounds that keep everyone happy. At the heart of it all, your priority should be the love and respect that a tolerant home demands.

43.

Don't Pick the Scabs

Injury arrives in many forms throughout a lifetime. Scrapes and scratches give way to bruised emotions and wounded egos. By the time we're adults in a healthy, romantic relationship, we're far more likely to suffer the pain of battling wills, little betrayals, and misunderstandings. Such wounds still hurt. They still take time to heal. And we're still compelled, just as when we were children, to pick at our scabs.

A wound requires cleansing. If you're hurt in the aftermath of relationship trouble, face it squarely, and confess it to your partner. You don't need to start a fight. It's enough to say, "When that happened, I felt this way, and I'm having trouble getting over it." In the best case, you talk it out, shed a few tears together, and forgive.

When you forgive, whether or not you ever actually forget the source of pain, you must allow it to heal. If you're still carrying the pain around—if you've got a scab that you keep picking—you have not exercised forgiveness. As long as you keep picking that scab, you'll continue to bleed. Forgiving the one who wounded you releases *you* from the offense and promotes your own healing. The physical metaphor can remind you to exercise some patience in the process, and you may hardly notice a scar.

An intimate relationship—especially a live-in partnership—inevitably includes disagreements, hurts, and struggles. What has happened once can happen again. When it does, it can act like a low-pressure system on an old wound. You may be healed and virtually never think of the old injury. Then one day the clouds arrive, the rain falls, and you start limping. There may be little or nothing you can do about memories and feelings that resurface at such times—but you can certainly choose to fight fair now.

Stick to the issue at hand. No one can constantly make reparation for every wrong or mistake that ever occurred in a close relationship. When you discuss new issues, resist every temptation to pick at old scabs. Repeat the process of admitting your pain, cleaning it up, and forgiving the source. Let old wounds throb if they must, but leave them alone and let them heal.

44.

Laugh Easily

In the face of life's stresses, laughter can lighten the load on your psyche. It helps you to take things less seriously and coaxes you out of a funk. When you smile, your body chemistry actually changes to chase off the blues or release anxiety. Laughter is no less helpful in a relationship. Just when you're ready to throw a shoe or dissolve into tears, you may catch an unexpected glimmer of just how ridiculous the argument is, and suddenly find yourself tickled.

Of course, laughter can be cruel or destructive, as well. There's a big difference between a good, old-fashioned knee-slapper of a traditional joke, and laughter at the expense of a person's self-esteem or dignity. Observe a few rules of thumb to preserve the blessing of laughter, and you'll make your life more joyful.

Laugh first at yourself. There's tremendous grace in the person who does.

Avoid teasing. Teasing as a source of laughter requires that you cut close to the bone. The humor resides in the truth behind the teasing. Sometimes the person you are teasing can take it on the chin and enjoy it, but it's not a risk worth taking. Too easily, you can touch a nerve and cause pain.

Always share the joke. The unexplained chuckle can be remarkably disconcerting. If you're amused by something that you're not willing to share, ask yourself why. It may be that you're wielding humor as a weapon or feeding negative attitudes. Laughter is only good medicine if you use it that way.

Let laughter express your deepest joys and greatest pleasures in your partner. A genuine ear-to-ear grin in the midst of shared good times is more valuable than a dozen assurances that you like and value the one you're with.

45.

Learn the Art of the
Strategic Retreat

We all have times when we need quiet and solitude more than anything. We may prefer to wake up slowly with our own thoughts. We may need half an hour of decompression after work or caring for children, before we're ready to relate to anyone. Or we may need a little time in the midst of a problem to cool off and think it through. Living alone provides such time and space free of charge. Living with a partner makes it less of a sure thing.

Small things can blow up into bigger problems when one or another life partner is suffering from a lack of solitude and emotional space. Often, unspoken signals specific to your mate will alert you to this need. Recognizing retreat as an option in such cases may save you some truly unnecessary upsets. But in fairness to both partners, there may be better ways to signal a need for solitude than the silent treatment, short answers, or a generally grouchy demeanor.

This is definitely a subject to discuss together when it's not an issue of the moment. People's needs for personal space vary greatly, and for a highly social, talkative person, a more solitary person's preferences can seem quite mysterious, and even a little hurtful. Once you've opened the door to discussing it, you also have the opportunity to figure out less stressful ways to communicate to one another when retreat is order. It doesn't take much to say, "I really need some space right now. Let's talk in a little while," or "This is a solo moment for me. Nothing to worry about." By agreeing that the need is legitimate and deciding how to communicate it when necessary, you give your partnership a great advantage and your mate a terrific show of respect.

46.

Lend a Hand Once a Day

You negotiate constantly in an intimate relationship. How much will each person contribute to shared expenses and income? Who gets the new car? Who decides where to go for an evening out? You negotiate as a means of expressing and sustaining your love for one another, seeking a balance that seems fair and mutually satisfying.

In your negotiating mode, you may look to see that each partner is treated equally. The relationship is all about fairness and peace. It's making an agreement, fine-tuning a contract. You might say that your life with your partner bears a close resemblance to a business deal in many respects. But the emotional intensity of an intimate relationship calls for much more than a good contract.

A relationship run merely on the basis of obligations met leaves a lot of room for doubt and disgruntlement. It's not that you aren't doing what you said you would. It's that you don't seem to care enough to do more. When this mindset exists between lovers, it can inflict a thousand tiny wounds that are impossible to pin down or address—but over time, they add up.

When you extend yourself beyond the agreed-upon and the expected of your negotiated agreements, you declare your love. Maybe it's just in offering to do a chore that's usually your mate's. Maybe it's in cleaning up your partner's mess, coming home with flowers for no good reason, or tracking down some tickets that mean a lot to him. The ways that you extend yourself beyond the negotiated deal will add up just as significantly as the ways you neglect. When you pour out affection, say not only, "I love you," but also, "Thank you for loving me."

47.

Be the Partner That
You'd Like to Have

S ometime in the past century, physicists came up with a startling idea. Later encapsulated in Heisenberg's Uncertainty Principle, it goes something like this: Because we live in a universe of relationships, we cannot study or observe any part of it as separate from other parts or from ourselves. In the simple act of observation, we have an effect. We change what we are studying *by* studying it.

In human relationships, we sometimes fall into the habit of seeing others and ourselves as fixed entities. At times, such an attitude serves us well. The traits or habits that might otherwise bug the daylights out of us are relegated to "the way a person is"; we give a philosophical shrug and move on.

But when the accumulated effect of these things leads to serious unhappiness, a fixed viewpoint of your mate, your relationship, or yourself becomes as problematic as the troubles that bothered you in the first place. You come to think that you can never be happy unless your partner changes. Yet you don't believe that's possible.

Consider Heisenberg's principle. Perhaps your partner refuses to budge. That doesn't mean that you can't change. According to Heisenberg, part of what you observe and experience is directly related to you. If you change, everything around you changes in relation to you. That includes your partner.

Obviously, the way you change will have ramifications. Decide to be the person—and the partner—that you want to be right now. If your unhappiness isn't defined, figure out what you want in your relationship. Don't let yourself off the hook until you know what you're looking for and what it will take to attain it.

Having done your homework, get busy. Identify just one way you can change how you think or act that will make you more the partner you want to be and wish you had. Practice it daily and self-consciously until it becomes the norm. Then incorporate another change, and so on.

There is tremendous satisfaction and power in taking responsibility for your own happiness. Furthermore, Heisenberg's Principle of Uncertainty comes home to roost as you change. Your partner cannot respond in the same way to a different person. When you change, your relationship changes. You can't lose, because you'll be transforming yourself into what you want.

48.

Find Reasons to Say
Thank You

When you love someone, you want that person to feel secure in your love and enjoy the peace that comes with that security. Yet you also want to know that you are appreciated, remembered, and understood. You want to hear "please" at the beginning of a request, and "thank you" in the wake of a kindness. Courtesy sends the message that you matter deeply to your mate. It is a way to demonstrate recognition that another person deserves your notice and respect.

Examine your current patterns and make adjustments. For starters, don't make it a habit to throw out the courtesies with the formalities. It's just as easy to relax when you remember to say please and thank you as when you don't. Taking on a mate means that you have two sets of sensibilities and requirements to keep in mind at all times. And part of keeping your mate in mind is demonstrating that you love and care through your thoughtfulness.

Different people of different backgrounds and upbringings may interpret courtesy in a variety of ways. Part of respecting your mate involves learning and respecting the courtesies that are especially meaningful to that partner. You can certainly practice the good manners that you find important for yourself, but broaden your horizons to include those that your partner cares about, as well.

Most of all, actively seek out opportunities to show courtesy to your mate. Notice just how many ways, great and small, your mate looks out for your feelings and interests, mention them, and say thank you. It doesn't matter if what your mate is doing is part of the deal you've negotiated with one another. The choice to be faithful to the agreement is itself worthy of thanks.

49.

Bend When the
Wind Blows

Conflict in a relationship can be a lot like the wind, showing up without warning and blowing with varying degrees of force. For a relationship to thrive despite the conflicts that hit like an unwelcome wind, you need to learn to bend in the face of the blow, as a tree does.

What does it mean to bend? It does *not* mean that you keep the peace at all costs. There are certainly conflicts in which self-esteem, a sense of fair play, or personal integrity requires a strong response. Bending also does not mean being "above it all." A condescending attitude toward your partner demeans your partner's pain and makes honest communication virtually impossible. Finally, bending does not mean going into hiding. It may be tempting to simply lay low with an eye to avoiding the work of dealing with a problem, but the next time that the winds of conflict blow, they'll give the problem added—and probably inappropriate—force.

What bending *does* mean is letting the first blast of conflict subside before you respond. When you feel you are under attack, you may want to quickly counterattack as a means of self-defense, or you may want to run away. These natural inclinations are called the "fight-or-flight instinct." Within an intimate relationship, this instinct rarely serves our best interests, because it has the effect of ending conflict at the cost of effective communication.

Bending means taking the time to let your emotions settle down after the blow has ended. Picture that tree as it's lashed by a blast of wind. It bends in one direction to keep from breaking, but eventually, it flies back in the opposite direction. Only when it has shivered to stillness does it return to good form.

Most of all, bending means keeping your inner being firmly planted in the reality of your cherished relationship. This takes regular mental and emotional exercise. Faced with your partner's criticism or temper, you may find it difficult to see the one that you love. But if you practice really seeing your partner in calmer moments, regularly noticing what you find lovable, and storing up that positive image, you have a resource for bad times. It helps you let go of your natural defensiveness and listen to what's really troubling your partner.

50.

Savor Every Bite

Too often, people neither notice nor appreciate individual moments or small pleasures in daily life. They pack as much into every day as possible, and then wonder why they aren't having a good time. As long as people continue to dash through their lives, they miss all the exit signs that could lead them toward better alternatives.

When people who overeat seek help in dealing with weight problems, they are often advised to look at their eating habits. Do they chow down while standing in front of the open refrigerator? Do they snack while they're preparing meals? Experts explain that by rushing the eating or distracting themselves while they eat, overeaters miss the emotional satisfaction that nourishing themselves should provide, which leads them to keep eating.

A day in your life can include a fabulous menu of potential nourishment. Some will be literal food, but some will be intellectual, emotional, relational, and spiritual. Your sense of satisfaction at the end of the day will depend less on how much or what you choose to fill the day with than on how you live it.

Overeaters are advised to plan each meal for nutrition and appeal. They transform eating from a frenetic act—self-medicating for boredom, depression, or anxiety—to one that offers nourishment for body, mind, and spirit.

It's hard to beat this formula for life in general. Start by planning what your day will be. Your physical being needs care and feeding. Your career makes specific demands. Your mate requires attention, as do children, pets, or other responsibilities that you've accepted. But most days also include discretionary time. Consider what will provide balance between activity and reflection, work and play, and responsibility and refreshment. A day that doesn't include items that recharge your spirit is an undernourished day.

As you live the day you've set out to accomplish, give thought to how you do it. If you're doing yard work, for example, do only that at that moment. Plan how much you will do on this occasion so that you have time to bring it to closure before you quit, even if it's simply one small stage of a larger plan. Then sit back on your heels and appreciate what you've done.

Giving this kind of consideration to each part of your daily life will transform it. When you take the time to plan, to be completely present in what you do, and then to savor it, you gain insights that help you to make a life that is not just full, but also fully satisfying.

51.

Take No Prisoners

It has been said, "All's fair in love and war." Unfortunately, if you conduct your love life according to this adage, love often turns into war. Nothing serves a loving relationship better than an underlying attitude of fair play, and nothing does more damage to trust and respect than the lack of it.

What makes for fair play in a relationship? It is predicated on a common understanding between partners. You must say, "This is okay, and this is not," on a wide variety of subjects. In a romantic relationship, matters of fidelity and honesty come to mind. How you handle disagreements, how you deal with in-laws or ex-partners, and how you share the load of the housework are questions that require consideration. Underneath them all is some agreed-upon set of standards that defines fair play—not only in general, but also for you in particular.

Stress arises between mates when such an understanding has never been addressed in the first place. In this case, the first thing that needs to happen is a time out while some rules and parameters are discussed. If you've never given some quality attention to the "rules" of your relationship, do it now.

Assuming that you have a mutual understanding of what constitutes your rules, consider this as an addendum: It's not fair to change the rules in midgame. If you believe that something needs reconsidering, make sure that you do it as a team. Changing an agreement requires the involvement and satisfaction of both parties.

In any relationship, plenty of issues arise that don't have a clear-cut answer, even in the context of a well-articulated understanding between partners. When something ambiguous comes up, work it out together with compassion and courtesy. In the same way, avoid the sneak attack: You have something to bring up, but you want to ensure that your partner responds according to your desires. You mention it while in company, making it awkward for your mate to disagree. This is a little piece of blackmail that will undermine the quality of your relationship in a hurry. While you're at it, take no prisoners. It's unfair to hold children, parents, or friends hostage to your desires.

The bottom line is this: Keep your primary relationship on the up and up. Then you'll have something solid and satisfying on which to build.

52.

Divide the Labor

Keeping a household running smoothly and with a minimum of stress involves management and cooperation. Even so, stress crops up over household matters, and no matter how small the issues, perspective can be hard to maintain when the irritations are staring you in the face every time that you come home. It's worth some creative action to keep these small matters in their place.

For example, when couples divide up their household labor in the early days of living together, they may decide who does what based on the traditions of their parents' households or according to perceived individual preferences and strengths. Often, however, these early decisions leave something to be desired. Perceived strengths turn out to be not so strong, preferences change, and the parental model doesn't apply by virtue of a different era, different personalities, and a different style of life. Stress develops.

Stress can also grow out of the simple human need for variety and revitalization. Household chores can be remarkably unrewarding.

Clothes are no sooner laundered than they are back in the hamper. The day after a good dusting, surfaces look fuzzy again. There's no keeping the kitchen sink free of dirty dishes.

Something as simple as periodically trading off household jobs can have a remarkably positive effect. It offsets boredom, brings a fresh eye to various chores, and gives each partner a greater appreciation for what the other does. You may create some fresh energy, as well, if you turn a solo job into a team effort from time to time. In addition to cutting the labor in half, you gain the pleasure of being together.

Maybe most invigorating of all—not to mention most loving—consider giving one another periodic vacations. One partner may agree to carry the whole load for a week. Or partners may decide that some part of the household work can go without attention for a little while. Better yet, if resources allow, a couple may want to hire someone to do what they usually manage themselves.

Whatever your solutions, keep household business out of the stress zone by giving it some creative attention. It's not worth fighting about.

53.

Take a Break

Time apart from one another can act as a great tonic for minor annoyances. Time at separate jobs or in different activities or organizations can certainly have some invigorating effects. So, too, can taking a course of study or getting involved in a community effort alone. But sometimes what's really needed is a true getaway—a vacation from your partner with no more complicated an agenda than refreshing yourself.

You may simply spend a day or a weekend in a favorite nearby city. Or you may travel to visit a distant friend or relative and enjoy some rare quality one-on-one time. Perhaps you could make a research trip that gives you fresh enthusiasm for your work life. Or you could go on a retreat of some kind, focusing on the life of your spirit and reconnecting with your beliefs.

Time apart has the remarkable capacity to put various aspects of partnership into fresh perspective. Your relationship can become confining without periodic forays outside of it. It's hardly surprising if you find yourself overreacting or feeling unidentifiable varieties of stress. When you venture out, tune in to a broader range of people, experiences, and concerns, and you'll rediscover yourself and your relationship as one small part of a larger reality.

Of course, there is a fringe benefit to separation, and that's reunion. Your first sight of the person you love can give you a glimpse of the person you first met and fell in love with. It can shift your attention to traits and peculiarities that you may ordinarily take for granted. And it can renew your delight in having someone with whom you share your life and love.

Just as you need a recharge once in a while, so does your partner. Offer your mate the latitude to take a breather, too. When you do, you honor your partner's separateness, you get a fresh view of home without your mate, and you gain the opportunity to create a homecoming that is a true breath of fresh air for your relationship.

54.

Change the Scenery

When the Impressionist artists first appeared on the scene in the second half of the nineteenth century, they startled the world with ways of applying paint and using color that had never been seen before. How did they take the stuff of ordinary life and traditional forms and transform it so remarkably? Underlying their new methods was a new perception. When they studied their subject matter, it was not the physical object that they concentrated on as much as the effects of light and atmosphere on the object. The physical object remained unchanged, but how it appeared, and how they represented it, differed with each change in the light reflecting from its surface and from the landscape surrounding it.

There is a strong strain of the ordinary and the traditional in an ongoing intimate relationship. You come to understand your partner and yourself in fixed terms and contexts. In many ways, the solid structure of who you are in relation to one another, and the conventions that go with it, lend strength and security to your relationship. But in other ways, you can become so tied to what you see as the objective reality—your perceptions of your separate identities, mutual concerns, histories, and plans for the future—that you lose the ability to flex and grow. You fail to see small problems in the making, and by the time the problems sneak up, you don't have the vision to see new possibilities and solutions.

Sometimes a new view of a familiar relationship or a problem requires a literal change of perspective. Change the angle from which you are looking at the relationship. Couples often get so immersed in the routines and the urgencies of everyday life that they fail to provide themselves with new vantage points. It takes less time and effort to keep doing what they've always done.

Consider your life as a couple. When was the last time you planned a getaway that required imagination and research? When did you last challenge yourselves by planting yourselves in an entirely new landscape? It's difficult to overemphasize the potential in creating a shared adventure on turf that is new to both of you. It doesn't have to be exotic or distant, but it certainly can be. Simply putting yourself in a different location from the familiar can shake up fixed perceptions and free you to have a new, creative view of your relationship.

A shared life needs a regular infusion of fresh ideas and perceptions if it is going to rise above the banal. When you give yourselves a new vantage point from time to time, you fuel your imaginations and revive your excitement in life and one another. Out of that can grow a quality and beauty of vision that transforms the ordinary and renews your perspective.

55.

Give More Than Necessary

Living together involves a fair amount of negotiation. Sometimes, though, this divvying up of a shared life leads to a mindset that makes too big a deal of keeping track. A fair division of labor becomes a scorecard, and equality in giving becomes tit-for-tat. As the years pass, you come to focus more on the dissatisfactions than the satisfactions. In the process, you lose all of the grace that can enrich a loving relationship and enlarge a human spirit.

How often do you give without any strings attached? How often do you give more than necessary? These involve a bit of extra effort. But when you do, you may find that you have greater resources than you realized. Not only that, you may find that your capacity to give actually expands because of the spirit in which you offer what you're giving.

Sometimes it's good to give simply because you can. Do something for your partner out of gratitude for one another. It's a sad thing to wake up alone one day with regrets about what you never said or did when you had the chance. Today is an opportunity that will not come again.

When you give, whether it's time, chores, activities, gifts, or kind words, give because you want to, and let virtue be its own reward. Then no one can disappoint you, because you're not looking for what you'll get in return.

Remember that giving is the essential language of love. You are privileged if you have someone with whom to share your life. Your relationship itself is a gift not to be squandered. Let your giving speak the love that you feel.

56.

Banish the Bogeymen

Fears can bear a strong resemblance to that bogeyman under your bed that you used to worry about as a child—more shadow than substance, and more daunting for remaining unexamined. If you don't take positive steps to address them, fears can become a frequent or constant presence in your life and love.

Are you afraid of what's going to happen with that big debt you and your partner have incurred? Do you worry about the health issues that you're observing in your parents and the potential ramifications for your own health in the future? Do you carry a fear that someone might discover you're a phony in one way or another? All of these are real fears that may or may not be justified, but toting them around like an old backpack only gets you stressed and unhappy.

Before you can do anything constructive about a fear, you have to admit that it's there and give it a name. In the case of the unpaid debt, for example, are you afraid of losing everything and being ejected from house and home by debt collectors? Are you afraid of

125

what the debt reveals about your or your partner's judgment or ability to provide? Perhaps you're afraid that others will find out that you don't have any financial substance. Giving your fear its true name is an essential step in getting beyond it.

Once you've seen the face of your bogeyman, it's possible to do something about it. In some cases, particularly when your fear has concrete sources, the next best step is to play out the possible scenarios and get further information. What are the bankruptcy laws in your state? Are there steps you can take now that will help you consolidate your debts? Suppose your friends find out. What do you honestly expect them to think or do? Do you really care about friends who would judge you for this?

Some fears have no real answers. Your father has a disease that has been shown to be hereditary in some cases. You fear that you may contract the disease, as well. Perhaps your fear can be allayed through more information, testing, or positive action. Facing the possibility of disability in the future with your partner and making contingency plans may help. In some cases, you may simply have to recognize that you don't know what will happen and choose to live fully and joyfully in the present.

There are frightening possibilities and uncertainties in every human life. We can live in bondage to those fears, or we can face them, let them go, and make the most of every day that we're given.

57.

Be Your Own Best Friend

In the long run, if you want to keep pettiness and hurt feelings in their place, your ultimate source of self-esteem needs to come from within rather than without. You may have constantly supportive friends and family, and your mate may be a miracle of affirmation. If so, you're one in a million—and even with all of that, you will face times when your fan club is unavailable or unaware. You may find that you have to make decisions or take actions that will not win you any praise. You must do what's right in spite of the lack of support you know you'll face. In the interest of integrity, you need to be your own best friend.

For many, this is one of life's greatest challenges. From the time we're children, we're encouraged to look to report cards, rites of passage, merit awards, and promotions to tell us what to think of ourselves. Relationships become our mirrors, and what we see in the reactions of others becomes our yardstick for self-appraisal. It takes conscious effort, reflection, and courage to move beyond that dependence to self-determination.

To begin, give yourself a break. You are a work in progress. At your best, you'll still make mistakes, do the wrong thing, or act too late, too soon, or not at all. You will be less than perfect—like every other human being.

Having accepted your limitations, give yourself credit. Imperfection does not negate the good qualities in you or the good work that you accomplish. Your worthy attempts deserve your acknowledgment and respect.

Perhaps most important to being your own best friend is taking care of yourself. Treat yourself the way you'd like to be treated by others and the way you'd like to treat your best friend. Make sure you are taking the time and effort to maintain healthy habits. Nurture your spirit with practices and observances that help you develop a moral life. Offer your mind good food to chew on. When you give your best attention to who you are becoming and what your life is really about, you will gain a growing appreciation of yourself and depend less on the reinforcement of others.

58.

Honor Your Secret Knowledge

An intimate relationship makes each of us a treasure trove of secret information about the other, from our dumbest mistakes to our deepest fears to our most annoying personal habits. We derive a measure of joy from knowing and being known. And we find some freedom and relief in the company of that special someone with whom we have let down the walls.

But the privileged information of a life partnership can also be a loaded gun, and you may get trigger-happy. Maybe you've got a gripe that you haven't resolved, and you welcome an audience to air it. Or perhaps you're just looking for good material to tell at a gathering, offering it as a funny story at your partner's expense.

Whatever your reason, you can be sure that you have put a hole in the fabric of your intimacy. No matter how supposedly insignificant or innocent the detail you've revealed, you've betrayed a trust. And there will be a price to pay, whether it's your partner's hurt feelings or your partner's decision to fight fire with fire.

When you choose to reveal your partner, you immediately put his dignity and self-esteem at risk. No matter how close you are, you can't climb inside your mate and feel his feelings or think his thoughts. Even when your partner chooses to join you in sharing secrets, you can't be sure that it means all is well. Often people cover their true feelings in the company of others out of regard for their comfort. They assume a façade of indifference, but they still hurt.

It could be that your partner is the one to start the stories about himself, and he encourages you to join in. Maybe some private subjects don't bother your partner. The trouble is that you can't know which subjects are the safe ones, nor can you know that the status won't change. What was okay yesterday may be a problem tomorrow.

There is only one way to honor the secret knowledge you have: Keep it to yourself. If your partner starts it, just smile and let him finish it. If others in a group decide to make secrets the order of the conversation, keep your mouth shut. If you're with people who love to dig up dirt, find ways to head them off—or consider keeping different company. When all else fails, find a reason to excuse yourself if you must. Most of all, take responsibility for using private knowledge as food for conversation. No one can make you speak about something. The power to speak or not is yours alone.

59.

Throw a Snowball

Your intimate relationship means the world to you. Nothing matters more than making it work. You earnestly apply yourself to being part of a solution, not a cause of a problem. Your efforts are worthy. And your relationship has no doubt benefited in ways that even you can hardly imagine. However...

Sometimes you may just be too serious. It's possible to overwork a project—even one that is at the top of your priority list. Good times and belly laughs can have as much positive value in a relationship as hard work and intensity can. Lighten up and allow fun to replace work every once in a while.

Just for fun, try going through one day with a metaphorical camera on your shoulder. Look at the lighter side of everything. The truth is that much of what you carry around as frustration or burden doesn't have a tenth of the weight you give it. All you need is a different lens to view it. Furthermore, you'll find the most laughable moments in what seems heaviest and most important.

Emotions become melodramatic. Gestures become larger than life. Granted, you should be careful about how you share a joke in a moment of melodrama. But just seeing it with a sense of the absurd is a move in a lighter direction.

Most important of all, let the good times roll. Give in to your playful impulses sometimes. Throw that snowball. Leave some time in your busy life as a couple for nothing more "productive" than play. Allow for spontaneity. The same playful spirit that energized your childhood lives on in you. You don't need to sit on it, even regarding the weightiest of matters. Fun is good. Play is productive. Laughter heals a tender heart and makes living sweet.

60.

Renew Your Promises

There was a time in the not-so-distant past when promises were taken very seriously. When someone said, "I give my word," that was considered to be as binding as a signed contract. But somewhere along the line, one's word came to mean less than the paper on which it was recorded. Today, ours is a culture of loopholes. These days, when people stand before God and witnesses and say, "Until death do us part," what they *mean* is, "Until death do us part...or until I change my mind."

The bottom line is simple. If you and your significant other mean what you've promised to one another, you will have to look to yourselves more than to anyone or anything else to support those promises.

In a couple's life, there are matters that call for serious intervention, and without remedy, these may be deal-breakers. But often you are faced with issues of far less magnitude that can and should be treated as part of the package to which you signed on. In fact, your promises have their greatest value when problems in your relationship loom large. For this reason, you'll do your partnership a big favor when you take your promises seriously enough to give them some regular care and feeding.

It could be profitable and affirming to pull out a written copy of the vows you and your partner exchanged and read them together. Maybe there are aspects to what you promised that bear discussion in light of the years you've shared together. Maybe some apologies are in order. What *did* you promise? What are the real-life ramifications of your words? Did you mean them or not?

You'll probably have some built-in opportunities not only to remember but also to renew your vows. Never underestimate the value of rituals in regard to the promises you've made. Anniversary celebrations, birthdays, religious observations, and other formal commemorations can add solemnity, sacredness, and awe to your renewal of promises.

Joining your life to that of another is a choice of magnitude. Your promises are the foundation of your partnership, intended to safeguard two hearts and the life they share. When the promises are strong and sure, you and your partner can concentrate on a shared life well and faithfully lived.

61.

Define Common Space

Some couples are lucky enough to have very similar personal habits, pet peeves, and preferences. A great many more find great challenges in the details of home life. Regardless of beliefs, goals, and values in common, they steam up over the way to squeeze the toothpaste or the proper place for dirty clothes.

Finding accommodations that both of you can happily live with is certainly the ideal solution to differences in style. Some couples become more similar simply by dint of living together and cease to feel the early tensions of being unique individuals thrown together. Other couples implement a bargaining style to get things done in their home. Each consciously gives way where they feel able and asks for extra consideration where they don't.

But sometimes these solutions just don't work. In such a case, a couple would be well-served to create a neutral territory—perhaps in an area of the house that would ordinarily be considered "public" space. Here, it often behooves the less particular partner to accept the need for order and cleanliness that the other partner feels. Of course, living together happily also requires fair play. It's only fair that the other partner be allowed some space where she can kick off her shoes, loosen her collar, and enjoy what is truly comfortable to her.

The key to building a positive life together is always the same: mutual respect. You don't have to change who you are to appreciate a partner who is different. You do have to exercise the will to serve both of your needs, expend the energy to find a satisfactory way to do it, and develop the compassion to truly desire as much freedom and happiness for your partner as for yourself.

62.

Take a Bird's-Eye View

When problems arise at home, we often believe that we can
see where the "truth" lies at the heart of the matter.
However, the truth between two individuals is never one thing. It is
a combination of facts, opinions, feelings, and perspectives. Your
"truth" may look nothing like your partner's. To really work out a
problem with your spouse, you must admit that the "truth" is
something you must share with each other.

One initial way to broaden your view is to take as careful stock
of your partner's position as your own. That means quieting down
sufficiently to have a sympathetic conversation. It means asking
non-threatening questions: "I don't really understand your point of
view here, but I really want to. Can you explain it to me?" It means
listening carefully. It also means continuing the conversation long
enough that your partner is satisfied that you have accurately
understood his position.

Seeing two sides of the conflict keeps you from holding too
tightly to one opinion or possible solution. Accepting that there are

two "truths" here will also help you put this problem in context. How big a deal is it relative to your relationship? What does it look like when you step back and consider it from a much broader perspective?

Give yourself and your partner some emotional distance. In the midst of stress, you may have a hard time seeing anything *except* the issue at hand. Take a break. Let tempers cool. Put the problem aside while you take a look at all that's good and productive in your life and relationship.

Remember why you're together and what you want as a couple. How does the problem you're experiencing fit into that picture? Is it a speed bump—a good reminder that you're moving too quickly or carelessly? Or perhaps it's a road sign that points to a needed *change* of direction. Then again, maybe what you're experiencing is one of life's hurdles—a challenge that requires a little more than average effort for a higher goal. Or maybe it's only the most minor of potholes. All you really need to do is move on.

In the context of an entire, loving life together, most daily tensions don't deserve the attention and angst we award them. Before you turn nothing into something, get a bird's-eye view. The present problem may not deserve the effort, but your relationship does.

63.

Plant a Tree

The plunge into "real life" does not have to spell the end of dreams in a relationship. The life of a couple is a stew that is always enhanced by the spice of new possibilities. When you dream together, you affirm that you look forward to a future together. You express hope in what that future will be and in your ability to have an effect on it. Furthermore, you can now bring to your dreaming more information than you had available when your relationship was new and untested. Your dreams have a firm basis in reality.

Take the time as a couple to go over the resources you're accruing for your future, and consider whether they serve your dreams. If you haven't begun any such planning, by all means, do so now. You don't have to have much to start. Putting aside a small amount at a time can develop into future resources for you and your mate that can make your dreams, or some version of them, possible.

Create a yearly ritual that celebrates your future. Maybe you'll want to actually plant a tree once a year. Planting a tree is an act that can signify new life, the renewal of resources, belief in the future, or care for posterity. Planting a tree speaks of love—for one another, for future generations, and for the planet. Formalize it with a toast, renewed vows, a meaningful reading from literature or sacred writings, or a statement from each of you that affirms your intentions. The act of planting a tree—whether literally or metaphorically—can become a regular reminder that you're in it together and that today does not define your possibilities and potential.

It's easy to get so caught up in the present that you can stop giving yourself the time and pleasure together to see visions of what is yet to come. It may present more of a challenge to restore dream time than to let it recede, but that doesn't mean you can't or shouldn't do it. The petty stuff of today loses its power in the context of hope for and anticipation of your tomorrows. Plant a tree together. Feed hope, and let it grow deep roots for your future.

64.

Retrain the Knee-Jerk Reactions

Any pattern repeated often enough—whether physical, mental, or even emotional—can become second nature. In sports, this can make for a winning game. In the world of emergency medical response, it can spell the difference between life and death. But in relationships, it can lead to trouble.

Many people have developed certain knee-jerk reactions. Sometimes they originate in childhood, at the hands of difficult parents, in light of traumatic relationships with other children, or in response to certain teachers. At other times, they grow out of adult experiences. They may have nothing to do with your history with your mate, or they may actually reflect past history with her. In any case, knee-jerk reactions have a nasty habit of either doing an injustice to an innocent person on the receiving end, or perpetuating destructive patterns with someone who played a part in your learned response.

Look for glib insults. Take note of quick jabs to the gut. Beware of instant steam. These are red flags of knee-jerk reactions. They happen predictably and instantly to certain stimuli—particular comments, actions, or situations.

Whether you identify a knee-jerk reaction in yourself or your mate, don't let it go. Point it out and talk about it. Get to the bottom of it, and make or accept the necessary apologies to clear the air. Give it enough attention so that you can no longer react in that way without thought. You might find it helpful to agree on a signal when the reaction crops up again—something that can remind you that you both know what is really happening and are moving beyond it *together*. Then look for new, positive responses to replace the knee-jerk reactions.

65.

Be a Haven

L ife is full of risk. We face challenges and fears associated with our families, our careers, raising children, and demands we may have from community involvement. Any of these can leave us feeling exposed and vulnerable. At such times, what you need most is a safe haven where you can regroup or rest. When you face risk at home, however, you might as well have sailed right back into a storm.

You can create an atmosphere of risk in relation to your partner without being aware that you're doing it. For instance, let's say your partner tends to run up high credit card bills, month after month. Such behavior can create a miserable sense of uncertainty for you. The money owed comes to represent more than financial insecurity. But the behavior also builds doubts about the spender's self-control, sense of responsibility, and loyalty to you.

When the next credit card bill arrives, you may let your frustration spill out: "You don't care about me at all." "I refuse to live this way." Such statements communicate the potential that in your view, the stakes couldn't be higher, and your partner's actions call for disastrous repercussions.

Now, if the credit card problem really is a deal-breaker, these statements are appropriate. They become a necessary wakeup call to your mate that to you, the issue is as big as they get. More often than not, however, such statements are merely threats that the angry partner has no intention of taking to the extreme. In this case, the anxiety produced in the spender is out of proportion to the reality. Again, your relationship becomes a danger zone rather than a safe area.

As a team, you and your partner can choose to make your relationship the safe harbor in each of your lives. This doesn't mean that you won't have issues with one another. It does mean that you refuse to let those issues take on monumental proportions.

Agree at the outset that whatever comes, you'll handle it as inseparable friends and lovers. Furthermore, stick to truthful, appropriate language when dealing with problems. Help one another by identifying the situations that make you feel vulnerable. When you know where the fears come from, you can work together to offset them.

66.

Keep the Back Door Open

You'll find a common thread in people who consistently make the most of what they've got. They are masters of the "win-win" situation. Instead of treating every confrontation as a contest, they see it as a concerted effort. Rather than aiming for the one-up position, they seek a team score. And in lieu of self-satisfaction, they accept compromises and creative solutions. They do it in their careers, in their communities, and most notably, in their relationships.

It sounds like a no-brainer, but when it comes to actual stress, you may find that your first instinct is hardly to hope for the win-win situation. In fact, many people find it nearly impossible to resolve a conflict without hearing or sensing "You win" from their partners.

Perhaps the single most important element for turning stress and arguments into a shared solution is the issue of saving face and retaining dignity. Webster's Dictionary defines "dignity" as "the quality or state of being worthy, honored, or esteemed." Too often, when you're intent on getting your way, you resort to tactics that demean, dishonor, or devalue your mate in some way. Your mate will respond naturally by defending his self-esteem.

Consider this scenario: Your partner asks for advice that he then ignores. When the result doesn't quite go the way he expected, you charge in with an "I told you so" attitude. Your partner cannot remedy the situation. His efforts are stymied by your self-righteous behavior. You've left no exit for your partner, no way of gracefully redeeming a poor decision or solving the problem with your help, as a team.

But suppose that you approach your partner in a different way. Rather than gloat, show him respect. Consider how you can make the most of his efforts, but then attack the situation as a team, perhaps applying some things that you originally thought would help him. Your partner's intentions and efforts are honored, his character remains intact, and you demonstrate your ongoing love and respect.

Keep the door open to charitable interpretations and win-win solutions. Aim for ways to save your partner's dignity when problems threaten. In the process, you will honor your relationship and indeed be a winner.

67.

Talk with Your Hands

Infatuation has an energizing effect on most people, and it tends to fuel their imaginations. But familiarity and external demands often slow people down. Security in a relationship can turn to complacency, and your loving actions may be taken over by a shorthand of words. When you're accused of neglecting your mate, you may fall back on "You *know* I love you!" But remember the old adage: "Actions speak louder than words."

Take stock of how you're showing love. Use a few minutes a day, even for just a week, to make a list of your loving acts. An inventory may highlight how infrequently you allow your actions to speak your love. But no relationship will thrive indefinitely in the absence of loving actions. If you've been remiss, don't let that defeat you. Get going now. Start by saying, "I'm beginning to realize how little evidence I give you of how important you are to me. Please forgive me. I'm going to do better."

Find some way every day to show your love, whether it's with household chores, social plans, or acts of kindness. Pay more attention to the ways your mate wants you to demonstrate your love. Actions as simple as making sure you return a tool to its proper storage place or adding toothpaste to the shopping list can say "I love you" more compellingly than the occasional grand gesture.

Don't forget that physical affection can send a powerful message. A foot rub at the end of the day, a bear hug in a moment of shared laughter, or an unexpected kiss on the neck can make a multitude of minor irritations shrink away to nothing. By keeping these tactile reminders of warmth and love in the mix, you affirm your love and your intention to be the other half of a team.

68.

Don't Sweat the Tides

We live in a world devoted to the quick fix. We hear it promised that for every challenge there is (or soon will be) a discovery, invention, or cure to meet it. We lose patience when the promises prove to be faulty or slow in coming. Only when we're faced with the awesome power of forces of nature such as the sea do we sit back and consider that sometimes we just have to wait something out.

Life has its seasons. People have their moods. Moods are natural. How you handle them affects how you face larger challenges. Moods are the tides of the sea in each of us. Respecting them as natural forces can lead you to wisdom.

First of all, understand that a mood is what it is. When your mood is dark, you may look for someone or something to blame. Let yourself off the hook—feelings in and of themselves are not right or wrong; they simply are.

It may be that you can make some external change that will turn your internal tide. Or your feelings may have no obvious cause.

In that case, remind yourself that moods come and go, and this one will pass. You can try not to heap negative thoughts on a down mood and try to lift your mood with exercise, the company of friends, or a change of scenery. However, some moods will not be hurried. Take heart—with a little patience, you can ride them out.

Remember, too, that the moody moments will most likely happen again. The more experience you have in refusing to take moods too seriously, the less power they have over your enjoyment of life and your partner. Call a mood a mood—"It's not you. I'm just feeling this way today." That way, no one needs to be burdened with an angry or fearful response.

69.

Do What You Love

Passion doesn't happen *to* us; it bursts from *within* us. We often recognize its presence when we fall in love. It feels so good that we regret its passing when it inevitably fades. For some, the desire to feel that passion again motivates infidelity in the midst of an ongoing relationship. For others, it leads to one short romance after another, without commitment to any single partner.

Happiness can certainly come from ongoing physical passion. But happiness that depends solely on sexual passion is limited, at best—it is vulnerable to the aging process, disease, separations, and moods. Passion that draws from a deeper reservoir has the potential to last a lifetime and bring a happiness that encompasses much more than the physical. If you want to make a life for yourself that is rich, vital, and fulfilling—especially in the context of a long-term relationship—you must consider passion without the expectations imposed by the media.

The longer you live, the more opportunity you have to discover what your passions are. There may be people who stir you at the deepest levels or causes that move you. A career or hobby may fire your passion, or your religious beliefs may set you ablaze. Any of these wake you up and motivate your most exuberant outpourings of energy and ability.

If you sense a lack of zip in your life, perform a fundamental assessment of how much room you allow for your own passions and how much energy you give to pursuing them. Only you know what wakes you up and keeps you ticking. And only you can make the decision to give your passions a prominent place on your priority list.

You don't have to seek out a new partner to feel a renewed sense of passion. Nurture a friendship that sparks your intellect or feeds your soul. You don't have to quit your current job to feel useful. Make up the difference in volunteer work, a compelling hobby, or ongoing education. When you do what you love, you transform your existence into a love affair with life itself. In turn, your happiness will spill over into your relationship. Instead of the dull sense that the happily-ever-after partnership you dreamed of is impossible in your affair, carry the torch you can light from the fire of your own passions.

70.

Honor Your Partner's Roots

If you are dealing with problematic in-laws, you must consistently distinguish between your partner and the extended family. You didn't wed them. Your partner didn't wed your family. The one you did wed deserves your loyalty and support, as you deserve loyalty and support in return.

If you have issues with your own family, make sure you understand the situation from your mate's point of view. If you have lifelong tension with your parents, for example, your partner may have strong negative reactions to them for the pain they cause you. Talk out the issues ahead of time, and be clear about how your mate can best support you in stressful family gatherings. And make a point of being your mate's most ardent defender in the company of your family.

Regarding your partner's extended family, you may avoid potholes by knowing ahead of time where to expect them. Ask how you can ease the time together for your partner. If the family doesn't appreciate you as the person of choice, you deserve your partner's full support. It's unfair to be expected to take it on the chin without backup.

Both you and your partner need to support one another in building a more compassionate view of your families. Make efforts to know them better. Ask them about their own lives. Make plans to meet one another in neutral territory and create some new traditions and memories. Honor their past, even as you ask them to accept your present. As you discover more about them, you may find more to like and respect. You may not become fast friends with them, but you may play a role in the family as a loving, supporting partner.

71.

Turn Down the Volume

Whether or not you realize it, constant noise in your environment constitutes a significant stress-producer. You may be so accustomed to it that you hardly take notice, but it takes a toll nonetheless—when some small annoyance comes up, you may not be at your peak performance in dealing with the problem.

There's little you can do about noise outside of your own home, short of petitioning for better sound pollution laws. But within the sphere of your control, you have choices that can reduce the noise in your life.

Just to begin, consider how many conversations with your partner take place over the background noise of a television or stereo. Half of the time, many people speak with one another while their eyes (and attention) flit back and forth between partner and TV screen.

Think of the effect of the telephone. Despite the potential boon of the answering machine, how often do you let the phone interrupt face-to-face interaction? A quiet evening together can be short-circuited by a friendly call that lasts too long or a total stranger looking to sell you something.

Nothing will give your relationship better growth potential than for you and your partner to be entirely present in the moment when you're together. Do yourselves a favor. Turn off the television when you talk. Let the answering machine get the phone once in a while. Set the table and light candles in lieu of TV trays. Sit together over coffee without the stereo in play.

You can choose to clean up the noise pollution in your environment. It may give you more peace of mind than you've had in a long time.

72.

Admit It!

If there's any lesson for all of us in the annals of human history, it's that we all make mistakes, we all suffer lapses of character, and we all share some portion of the blame some of the time. This is no less true in a romantic relationship. Life with another human being always includes some pain, mistakes, forgetfulness, and mismanagement.

Inevitably, people let one another down on occasion. He promises to pick up an extremely important package at the delivery center, then completely forgets to do it. She is depending on him and will miss a deadline as a result. She expresses her acute disappointment and frustration, only to be met with a list of angry excuses and reasons why he forgot—she didn't call to remind him, and he was doing her a favor, after all. Now, on top of her initial frustration, he has added insult to her injury by making her the bad guy—she feels attacked for her original innocent request. He has recast his broken commitment as her selfishness, and sparks really begin to fly.

Suppose instead that he had unveiled the emotions he was *really* feeling when he realized that he had inadvertently broken his promise: embarrassment, guilt for the trouble he had caused her, anger at himself. Suppose he had chosen to then apologize and had offered to do whatever he could to help her repair the damage that had resulted. A decent, compassionate person would accept his apology, admit that we all make such mistakes, and let him do what he could to help. An incident that could blow up and leave a legacy of hurt will have become one more building block in understanding one another and working together for the good of both.

The moral of the story is this: Even big issues can be tamed into manageable, positive experiences. When you're in the wrong, there is high ground available. You can reach the heights in three firm steps. Admit responsibility. Ask for forgiveness. And make whatever amends are possible. Even if your partner does not offer forgiveness and acceptance, you will have the satisfaction and comfort of having done the right thing.

73.

Delete "Failure" from
Your Vocabulary

What is failure, really? Is it an attempt that did not work? Is it a dumb decision, a thoughtless act, or a misspoken word? Too often, you can walk away from a failed effort, misjudgment, or actual wrongdoing with a giant "F" emblazoned on your self-esteem. You cease to distinguish yourself from the behavior or attitude that went awry. In your own eyes, you *become* a failure.

Self-reproach has destructive power that is hard to overestimate. Every small mistake bloats with the weight of self-indictment. You may cease trying for fear of future failures. You can become bitter and cynical about others. Good things that happen to other people arouse envy. You hold your mate and yourself to impossible standards and make both of you miserable.

Creating a life that rewards your efforts requires a learning curve. In fact, it's the nature of life that you learn through trial and error over time. In our own era, there are many examples of gifted individuals who consistently did poorly in school and heard that they wouldn't amount to much. Albert Einstein flunked math. Thomas Edison endured thousands of failed experiments and several bad business enterprises. But their later contributions had widespread effects. They represent countless others who view the mistakes in their lives as grist for the mill. Instead of seeing themselves as losers when one course of study or action isn't working, they let that experience guide them toward a better choice.

The vocabulary of success and failure is loaded. Hit the delete button when those words of judgment settle into your thinking. You and your mate, like the rest of us, are in a state of becoming. Error is all part of the process.

74.

Listen with Your *Other* Ears

Living with another person can make that person's voice and reactions so familiar that you can come to listen with only half an ear or tune out the voice altogether. Only when a major upset over something small doesn't "compute" are you alerted to the fact that you may have missed something important along the way. You need to listen with something other than your ordinary ears.

An overreaction usually erupts for a solid reason. Of course, physical lows certainly have the power to shorten fuses and drain coping skills. It is almost always worth risking further fury to ask, "Are you feeling all right?" If your mate confesses, "I have a miserable sinus headache," you respond with sympathy and some decongestant, and all is well.

But maybe your question is answered with a curt "I'm just fine," and a slammed door. Dismiss the easy solution and keep listening. It's possible that the reason for the overreaction bears little or no relation to the precipitating event of the moment. Rather it is displaced emotion that was not handled in relation to its true cause, but has poured out after a minor irritation opened the floodgate.

At times such as this, take a giant step back. Adding your own overreaction to that of your mate will only get you into a pointless fight. Answer a too-big reaction with calm and balm. If the precipitating event was your doing, make a point of apologizing—and mean it. The fact that your mate responded poorly doesn't excuse the fact that you did something thoughtless or unkind. At the same time, express your surprise at the *size* of the response. Your mate may not even realize that his reaction was over the top.

At this point, you can ask if something else in the relationship might be the real fuel behind the flash point. Listen between the lines to ferret out why this problem is important to your mate. Watch for indications of what it might represent to him—a lack of love, a pattern of selfishness, or larger anxieties.

It's always possible that the emotion behind an overreaction to you actually grows out of anxiety, anger, or hurt that has nothing to do with you. It can be useful to open the door to such a revelation by asking, "Is there something else bothering you?" For all you know, you missed something in your partner's life that deserves your attention. If you make yourself available, you may find that you have a valuable listening ear to offer.

75.

Tend to Your Business

Scores of books, magazines, web sites, and television shows are produced on the subjects of making and investing money. In addition, a growing corps of accountants and brokers offer their services for reasonable fees. But whether or not you seek help, you will almost certainly run into money stress unless you take time to plan and maintain the financial aspect of your partnership.

First of all, tend to the business side of your relationship as a team. Keep the subject of money on the table. Plan monthly meetings in which you review how you're doing and make any changes or decisions that affect how you go forward. Don't let your financial picture slip out of sight and mind. It's too easy to have problems when you neglect this fundamental aspect of modern life.

Make sure both of you understand your financial situation. It's fine to delegate the business of paying bills or balancing accounts, but that's no excuse for ignorance on each other's part. You both need to review the bills and be up to date on all of your balances. Knowledge will help you make smart decisions.

Create a budget together that accurately reflects your resources, your goals, and your priorities. Set money aside for fixed expenses, charitable commitments, and long-term savings and investments *before* you set limits on discretionary spending. A well-thought-out, realistic financial plan can remove an enormous amount of anxiety and friction from a couple's daily life.

Finally, help one another live within that budget. If you support one another in living according to your budget, you immediately offset the worst money problems that may regularly arise between partners.

76.

Institute the "Time-Out" Strategy

All couples have their arguments. Given human nature, at least some of the arguments are probably inevitable. Your best defense is to learn how to manage them so that they are resolved as quickly and painlessly as possible.

When an argument arises, first consider whether it has occurred at a time and in a place in which it can be resolved productively. Generally speaking, public places are not good settings for settling disputes. Neither are family gatherings or the hallway outside a "sleeping" child's bedroom. Any time or place that adds extraneous issues such as listening ears, other activities (sleeping, making love, or eating, for example), or embarrassment to the original conflict calls for a definite "time out." In the same vein, if you see that tempers have already made a reasonable resolution impossible, back off for a spell. Declare a truce until your blood pressure and your sense of proportion return to normal.

When you go back to the conflict, agree to stick to the issue. Take time for each of you to voice your view and your idea of a good resolution. Avoid yelling; the louder you shout, the less likely your partner will hear you. Avoid global statements ("You always..." or "You never..."); you'll only increase the stakes. And avoid sneak attacks. If you verbally back your mate into a corner just to prove she's wrong, the fight-or-flight instinct is aroused and invariably either escalates or ends the discussion.

When you reach a resolution, agree to let that be the end of it. If either of you brings it up, give the other permission to cry foul. Arguments may be unavoidable, but you can learn to deal with them in ways and at times that keep them as small as they ought to be.

77.

Be Ready for Bright Ideas

You and your partner are people in process, and your relationship is a dynamic expression of that process. Your circumstances continue to evolve. Your family members age and transform. Your circle of friends grows and shrinks and grows again, as do the demands on each of you and your relationship.

Use your view of others to learn. You are surrounded by couples at various stages of life with a wide and often disparate range of experiences. They include your own parents, extended family members, and friends. They may include neighbors, colleagues, or members of your community groups.

Not that you should believe all that you see or hear about others' partnerships, but there are observations to be made. The company of a couple who consistently treat one another with affection can offer hints on how to promote such a climate in your own relationship. Conversely, time spent with a couple who always bicker can remind you of the pettiness of such a style.

Books, interviews, and lecture series can offer helpful insights on a variety of topics such as communication styles and sexual issues. Sometimes you may feel a need that compels you to research a topic, but you don't have to wait for trouble. You can gather solid information about the challenges that typically surface in a partnership before you face such challenges yourself.

Perhaps the most difficult wisdom to embrace is the timely observation or sage suggestion from someone outside of your relationship. Yet someone with more experience and wisdom worth sharing may see what you don't. When you're offered advice, you don't have to accept it, but you should examine it.

78.

Nurture Your Body

We're quick to ascribe psychological explanations to our outbursts and overreactions. Unfortunately, we often leave our physical state out of the equation. Yet the evidence is in. If you want to increase the balance, peace, and joy in your life, remember the importance of regular attention to your physical health.

If you've never had a physical examination by a licensed medical practitioner, do it now. The best medicine is preventive, and before you get carried away with other issues of health, you should know where you stand. At the same time, run your own maintenance check on your lifestyle and habits. People sometimes get so caught up in their daily lives that they forget how much of an impact these factors can have on how they cope.

Do you get enough rest? The common wisdom on the subject suggests that most individuals need about seven to eight hours of sleep a night. Many doctors recommend a mid-to-late-afternoon rest, whether it's a twenty-minute nap or simply a short period of quiet. Well-rested, you refresh your mental and emotional resources and keep your sense of balance and proportion.

How about exercise? Taking several good walks a week has been shown to significantly benefit heart and lung performance. But many people find that regular physical activity offers more than cardiovascular fitness. They feel more energetic, better able to concentrate, and happier.

Good nutrition fuels your entire system. Including a disproportionate amount of processed foods, sugar, alcohol, and high-cholesterol protein sources will take its toll over time and displace the more healthful effects of whole-grain foods, fruits, vegetables, and low-fat proteins.

Maybe all of this sounds like a lot of work, but it isn't so much labor as it is habit. You already have routines. Just rethink them with your physical well-being more firmly in mind. Above all else, learn how to relax. Physical tension translates quickly into stress and anxiety. Relaxation techniques are available and attainable to anyone willing to apply them.

79.

Nourish Your Spirit

It's easy to get caught up in appearances in a culture that places so much emphasis on the shapes and sizes of our bodies, the jobs we hold, and the material goods we own. But to make a life meaningful and joyful, you must give some quality attention to the life of your spirit—that aspect of your existence that has to do with God, faith, character, integrity, and morality. There is no substitute for this facet of life, because it is here that you will find your compass for all else. It is here that you discern the difference between what is temporary and what lasts, what is superficial and what is important. It is here that you learn who and what you value most.

For many, spiritual nourishment comes most significantly in the context of religious beliefs and experiences. Actively seeking a connection to God affords a spiritual yardstick against which to measure decisions, consider moral issues, and build a life of integrity with your mate. Faith can grow in the context of a commitment to a religious community, to rituals and observances that highlight aspects of your beliefs, and to regular habits of study, prayer, and meditation.

On a more human scale, the spiritual side of your life can also be served by the arts. The visual arts, music, drama, literature, and dance can speak to the fire within you, moving you beyond your usual boundaries of conversational language and logic. The arts offer you beauty, charge your creativity, and challenge your way of seeing.

So, too, does the natural world. In nature, you will discover some of the most powerful and poignant pictures to be found, of cycles and seasons, balance and interplay, life and death. It's easy to lose your sense of proportion when you focus on one tiny facet of your personal life. In nature, we're reminded that life is *never* one thing, but always a magnificent web of many things in constant motion and connection. Study the galaxies or observe life under a microscope if you want to put yourself and your life into a larger picture. The more we sense what is all around us, the more we understand the limits of our humanity. Such humility is the beginning of wisdom.

80.

Exercise Your Intellect

As partners in life, you can reinforce small-mindedness in one another. You can fall into dull habits that rarely or never take in new ideas or alternative perspectives. You can keep subscribing to the same periodicals with the same biases and listening to the same commentators with their same partisan points of view. You can also indulge one another in a diet of junk food for the brain. How many television shows do you really believe offer intellectual challenge? What sort of mind-stretching does the average popular movie require? Does your literature provide you with any food for thought?

You can also be one another's motivation to exercise and feed your intellects, broaden your outlooks, and move beyond what is easy and comfortable. There are probably as many ways to do this as there are couples with options and imaginations.

Turn off the television at least once in a while—just for one day a week, or for a week out of the month. Television numbs the mind and displaces many alternative sources of interest and challenge.

Even as an agent of relaxation at the end of the day, it might be profitably traded in for a great piece of music or a spicy meal.

Read a book or listen to one on tape together. Pick out something that appeals to you both. Good books give us something to chew on and discuss. They teach us about people, events, places, times, and experiences. They give us new territory to explore together.

Put yourselves on a learning curve. Studies have shown that the effects of aging on the human brain are substantially offset when a person continues to learn. Take on a new course of study or a different hobby, or try to attain a higher level of skill in one of your areas of expertise.

Remember to keep yourself in the mix. When you involve yourself in venues where there is multigenerational or cross-cultural participation, you broaden your range of exposure. People of different generations or cultures have different contexts out of which they view life and the world. Mixing with different people gives you the opportunity to step into other experiences and see through new eyes.

81.

Share Your Offspring

A library of books couldn't begin to cover all of the issues involved for couples seeking to raise children together. There will be many daily trials that can be negotiated with grace and perspective or inflated into trouble that serves no one. In aiming for grace and perspective, consider four simple suggestions:

Stand united. Love for your offspring can make you unusually headstrong in your opinions, and your opinions will not always agree with those of your mate. However, it's critical, for the sake of your children, that your differences be handled without involving them. Work together as you develop your family style. Join forces on discipline. Postpone decisions on which you cannot agree, and work them out in private. Stand behind one another's decisions. Leave your children in no doubt that you are a parenting team.

Be consistent. When children are given clear boundaries that they know will not change, it gives them an indispensable sense of safety and security. When you set rules, maintain them. Don't lower the boom for something one day, and ignore or laugh at it the next. When a situation or a particular behavior calls for a new rule, make it simple and clear. Spell out the consequences for disobedience ahead of time. Follow through. Remember that your children will learn more from what you do and how you do it than from what you say.

Share the load. Children demand an enormous amount of time, energy, and attention. When you bring them into the world, you and your partner assume a responsibility that will in some ways remain with you for the rest of your lives. It's not the work of only one of you to see that responsibility through, even if you choose to have one parent stay at home. When you carry the load together, you halve the stress and double the fun.

Love it while it lasts. Those children are with you for a remarkably short time. Many parents, when all their children have left, look back on the exhausting, volatile, exciting years of raising the kids as some of the best years of their lives. While you're still in the middle of them, cherish every day.

82.

Honor Your Own Roots

You face a challenge when you commit yourself to someone and, in effect, create a new family. Your new family takes precedence because it is with this other person that you must build and negotiate an adult life. But the act of starting a new family doesn't mean that your family of origin just vaporizes.

Most people want a continuing relationship with their relatives, but it isn't always easy. If you are on wonderful terms with your extended family—if you have found a balance of time spent together, your mate enjoys them as much as you do, and they have fully accepted your mate—count your blessings. Let it be one of the great supports for a happy, meaningful life with your partner. For the rest of the population, a few fundamentals may help to minimize the stress that can build.

Give your mate your first loyalty. Anything less is unfair and eventually disastrous. You've committed yourself to your partner and made promises that you need to honor. You cannot thrive in this relationship if you allow your parents, siblings, or others to come first. Your partner has a right to have some say in the part your family will play.

Honor your roots. Remember that in most cases, the people who raised you did the best that they could. They made mistakes, to be sure, but they loved you and meant the best for you, whether or not they knew how to accomplish it. Forgive them their faults. Seek to repair lingering resentments. Most of all, be an adult in relation to these people. You're old enough now to understand and get over your childish ideas of them.

Seek to build alliances. If you adopt a compassionate, loving view of your family, your mate can learn to do so, as well. Alternatively, your family is not the best audience for your complaints about your mate. Emphasize your partner's strengths and lovable qualities to your family to help them understand and accept the person you've chosen.

Most of all, be thankful that you have family. Not everyone does. Take advantage of the time you have to learn more about where you come from. Make the effort to make amends and resolve old conflicts while you can. Let them know what you admire in them before they are no longer available to hear it. The aggravations are not as important as the bonds that you share.

83.

Maintain Some Mystery

There is great comfort and strength in having someone to have and to hold through all of life's ups and downs. But that kind of intimacy does not necessarily demand total exposure at all times or in all ways. It is possible to be emotionally honest and deeply committed without throwing every detail of your private existence in your partner's path. In fact, some aspects of your private life can be kept to yourself *in order* to keep your partnership vital and interesting.

Consider, for example, the issue of dirty clothes that are left in a heap at the end of a day instead of being put in a hamper. In your own home, you might think that you should be able to drop your clothes where you take them off if you want. On the other hand, if your partner finds such evidence of your disrobing more annoying than sexy, what are you accomplishing by digging in your heels on the subject? You might consider hiding the evidence in the interest of making bedtime (and the morning after) more alluring to your partner, and thus more pleasurable for both of you.

So, too, with a myriad of daily habits: When you stop thinking or caring about your partner's reactions to your everyday, nitty-gritty choices, you treat your partner as something less than the object of your romantic interest. In effect, you say, "I don't really care anymore how I appear to you."

Maintaining some mystery in your relationship depends most on being alive and in the moment with your partner. In a bad mood, your partner may register a complaint about something you routinely do or don't do. That's something to note, but it may call more for a moment's compassion than a permanent change in behavior. However, a complaint may be a reminder that you've become careless about the person you are when you're with your partner. If so, you may need to give some serious thought as to how you can return to a more romantic version of the intimacy you share.

Romance dies without care and feeding. One way to nurture that aspect of your relationship is to keep some mystery in the mix. Do some of your primping in private. Pay attention to the particular habits that your partner might prefer not to witness. And make a point of putting your best self into play for the one you call your intimate. You'll add the pleasures of new love to the depth of mature relationship.

84.

Promote Pillow Talk

It's tricky to introduce the subject of sex into any discussion. One or both partners in an intimate relationship is almost certain to be offended. Sex is a big issue in intimacy, and it's one of the two most prominent problem areas (along with money) that arrive on the therapeutic couch. If you're experiencing any sort of stress in the bedroom, there's no substitute for talking about it.

As in other areas of your relationship, you cannot assume that your partner knows what you are feeling or understands why. Unless you express yourself, you may wait a long time before your unhappiness is detected. Keep in mind that sometimes sexual problems are the result of physiological problems, and talking may need to be the first step toward seeking medical help. But more often, problems with sex reflect other problems between partners. In that regard, the sex stress is part of an alert system that can work to the benefit of your relationship. It signals that you have issues that need to be put to rest.

Begin on a mundane level. You may simply need to give yourselves more relaxed time alone. Many couples fall into dull, infrequent sex because of too many commitments, weariness, lack of privacy, or anxieties over issues unrelated to one another. A night together away from home, a vacation without children, or a deliberate change of pace at home alone can get the engines revving anew.

Troubles may run deeper, of course. Some sexual issues loom large enough that you can't seem to work them out between the two of you. Don't despair or give up. Many people run into intimacy problems that they can't resolve alone. There's no shame or failure in that. Happily, you don't have to go it alone. Much help is available in the form of professional counseling, sex therapy, and literature on the subject. The more you know, the better equipped you'll be to work through problems and revitalize this part of your intimate life.

Perhaps most of all, on a day-to-day basis, allow your sex life to be what it is—an incomparable heart-to-heart about just how much you love one another. Don't tie it up with a hundred other strings attached to it. Don't make it an ordeal, a test, or a duty. Think of it as you would dessert. Make it the great treat it's designed to be.

85.

Make Meals into Dates

Everything seems to happen in a hurry these days, and every couple has its own set of time challenges and pressures to consider. But all people have one or two things in common. For instance, they need to sleep and they need to eat.

Sleeping together can be immeasurably pleasurable at times, but for the most part, it's the time when you're unconscious. In terms of time together to regroup, eating deserves some attention. It used to be the cultural norm that a family sat around a table at the same times daily and ate together. Many families today are lucky if they find even one night a week when they're all in at the same place long enough for a single dinner together. But this is a choice that can be changed.

Begin by considering how many times a week you actually eat together. Of those times, how many of your meals are catch-as-catch-can? How often do you stop long enough at the table to sit over *empty* plates and chat? Do you ever let your answering machine take the calls for an hour? How often do you do other things while you eat—watch television, read, or do paperwork?

The answers to these questions can have a profound effect on whether you even want to sit together over a meal. Food is more than nutrition. It's nourishment for your soul. Mealtimes have great potential for quality time and conversation. But first, you have to reclaim them from the hurly-burly of high-speed modern life and treat them as the special occasions that they can be.

Perhaps one or both of you enjoys cooking. In that case, make meal preparation a significant part of your time together. Make regular dates to try new recipes. Maybe you enjoy a certain kind of "take-out" food at the end of a long work week. Maybe you love a farmer's breakfast on Saturday morning. Don't fall into the trap of thinking that the only time you can have a date over a meal with one another is when you go out to a restaurant.

The point is this: The stuff that makes life sweetest requires down time. Many of us declare that we can't fit one more thing into our crowded lives. Fine. Then reclaim one aspect of life that you have to include anyway. Make dates of meals. Turn them into slow time when you can remember how good life can be and how glad you are to have the partner that you have.

86.

Once a Month, Trade Jobs

If you can actually accompany your partner through a typical day or trade places, by all means, do it. But you also can and should make a regular practice of asking about your mate's typical workday. Every so often, devote your attention to what your mate is experiencing, thinking, and feeling about work.

Keep in mind a few tips for making the most of this opportunity. First, refrain from saying, "I know." You don't know. If you're especially sensitive, *maybe* you can imagine. But you'll show more support if you choose a response such as, "That must really be hard for you," or "How do you feel about that?"

Second, resist the temptation to immediately relate your mate's experiences to those of your own. It's remarkably easy to rush into a tale of your own and take over the discussion. For the duration of one conversation, let the topic be your partner.

Third, reserve judgment. You may secretly think that you have the tougher row to hoe. No matter how hard you try to hide it, harboring such an opinion will diminish your capacity for empathy. That little judge will be sitting silently in the back of your mind with a snide smile, dubious and superior. You won't really hear or understand your partner's life from that point of view.

Finally, exercise your loving imagination. You hold the privileged position of being your mate's primary support. If you're willing and exert the effort, you can lift some of that load simply by honestly feeling the weight *with* your partner and standing alongside. It's always easier to face the hard aspects of daily work when you feel sympathy and understanding from another person.

87.

Volunteer Together

You may focus a lot of attention in an intimate relationship on your individual and mutual needs and how well they are being met. In the process, you can sometimes develop such a myopic view of life that you become not only the center of your universe, but the universe itself.

There comes a time when you have to stop staring into each other's eyes and look outward instead. This isn't to say that you should cease to make one another your top priority or neglect opportunities to care for the needs of your partnership. It is to say that you will regain your perspective when you choose to stand shoulder to shoulder instead of nose to nose. You become a team with a shared mission instead of a secret society of two. You'll understand yourselves as one small partnership in a much broader framework. You're not the whole show.

Much has been said in recent decades about the effectiveness of grass roots efforts and local involvement in community and social concerns. Nothing can take the place of ordinary people pulling together and helping out. Whether they're instituting "cleanup" days to collect litter, operating soup kitchens to help the hungry, or holding orphaned infants in hospital wards, people give their time and talents just for the satisfaction of helping. You can, too.

It's hard to be self-absorbed when you're focused on the real needs of others. Interestingly, when you shift focus as a team, you'll often find that the concerns that have troubled you begin to recede. You'll have less energy for pettiness, more appreciation for what you have, and a broader range of shared experiences that help you grow together in the same direction.

You don't have to do something enormous in order to make a significant volunteer contribution. Sitting on the public library board for a year can keep a worthy organization in top form. Collecting blankets at the holiday season and dropping them off at a distribution center can help people who don't have enough. Donating clothes to a charity may help a runaway youngster to have a second chance.

You won't need to look far to discover what humanitarian, conservation, and preservation efforts are afoot in your region. Local chambers of commerce have a complete listing of charitable groups. Check with the churches in your community, as well. You don't have to sign on to anything huge and time-consuming. It's enough to be a small part of a big effort.

88.

Sort, Dispose, and Donate

We live in a time of plenty. Our homes are designed for maximum storage potential, and we make sure we fill them up. We have at least one car for every driver in the household and a television in every room. We buy separate tools or appliances for every function and new outfits for every occasion. In fact, most of our homes are bursting at the seams.

Material consumption is a choice. So is the clutter that inevitably follows. You can relieve yourself of some of your stress by divesting yourself of some of the stuff.

Pick a trouble spot that you know is full of stuff—maybe the hall closet. Agree with your partner to set aside a couple of hours to empty that closet. When the time comes, sort the entire mess into three separate piles: stuff to keep, stuff to toss, and stuff to give away.

The stuff to toss is easy. Small trash just goes into the barrel. Recyclables are handled according to the regulations of your town or region. Larger items immediately take a quick ride to the dump.

With the tossed items gone, do a second sort of the giveaways. There are many charitable organizations that collect items for people in need. Or you may personally know someone who has a need for something that you are no longer using. Pack up the items according to what you're doing with them and deliver them as appropriate *within the week.*

Now you're down to the keepers. Look through these items one last time. Do you or your partner really want every one of them? Are there any items that really don't belong in that particular closet? If so, move them to a more logical storage space with other items like them.

At last, you're ready to restore the closet. Two final questions just for the fun of it: Could you organize the closet more efficiently so that the items are easy to see and access? If so, why not do it now, while you're at it? Install any shelves, drawers, or hooks. It will be worth the effort to make that closet a simple, satisfying corner of your home.

The process you've just gone through can be repeated in virtually any space in your house. Doing it as a team allows you to make decisions on the spot—no stashing stuff away until you can get your partner involved. Too much of a good thing can weigh you down. Lighten up.

89.

When in Doubt, Make Up

Everyone goes through times when they see their partners through less than adoring eyes for no particular reason. It comes out of weariness, boredom, or a bad mood. It erupts in times of personal doubt and change. You can make it into something big and scary, or you can face the fact that we're all human and go from there.

Don't let the occasional dip in your feelings for your mate set you up for trouble. It's important to remember that loving and liking are not always synonymous. Loving has to do with much more than romance, and principal among the ingredients is commitment. When you take on a life partner, you accept a whole package, not just the adorable options. And sometimes, through no fault of your mate's, the stuff you're not so crazy about seems to be the most prominent.

When your partner is simply "getting on your nerves," do what you least feel like doing. Instead of picking on the first annoyance that comes up and turning it into a complaint, find something specific for which you can genuinely thank or praise your mate.

When you're tempted to pick a fight or actually find yourself in the process of doing so, turn it on its head by admitting that you're at fault before the fight has time to develop. Apologize for taking out your funk in a way that is making your partner suffer. And move on.

When you feel the greatest yen to grab the next flight to anywhere away from your mate, choose that moment to make a date with your partner. It can be as simple as a long walk on a beautiful day or as complicated as a weekend away. Don't load the occasion with great expectations or false romance. Just act on the commitment you've made in love.

When a bad mood strikes, it can easily become self-sustaining. But you can take responsibility for changing the direction in which you're moving. By taking positive action toward your mate in response to negative emotions, you can actually turn the tide. When those ill-defined lows strike, strike back. When in doubt about why you're picking on your partner, make up.

90.

Listen Between the Lines

There is a particular sting to the criticism you receive from your partner. You may respond defensively because the source of the criticism is threatening to your self-esteem. If you're going to keep your balance and remain open to understanding, the trick is to listen between the lines. Most criticism happens on more than one level with a mate. There's the complaint against you, and then there's what it signifies to your partner. Generally speaking, it's the latter that allows you to put the complaint in perspective and do something about it.

There are several steps to handling criticism constructively. As a first step, say something like, "Tell me again exactly what is bothering you." Remain calm and hear what is said without the distortion of anger or surprise.

Once you know what the complaint is, continue with, "Please explain why this is a problem." In essence, you're asking for further clarification. Many "problems" are not objectively problematic issues. You need to know what lies behind them before you can say with sincerity, "Oh, now I get it."

Now, maybe you understand the complaint completely and feel from the outset that it's justified. In that case, this might be your opportunity to simply apologize. It is amazing how quickly an apology can take the wind out of the sails of a complaint. Your mate feels understood. You feel mature.

As a final step to resolving a matter, ask your mate, "How can I do better?" Responding one step further can reinforce the fact that you take your mate seriously. Maybe you won't like what he suggests. Suggest something else. Keep trying until you find common ground that puts the matter to rest.

91.

Test Your Judgment

What do you do when some of your issues have grown out of control? The arguments and conflicts come to bear an appalling similarity to one another. Each time they surface, you each retreat farther into your corners and slowly lose hope for any resolution. You wonder how long you'll go on like this before you can't stand to do it anymore.

If you're involved in such a relationship, reconsider your thoughts and actions. A frozen relationship robs everyone of joy, peace, satisfaction, and promise. When both parties refuse to budge and all attempts have failed to break down the walls, drastic action is required. You must seek help.

Professional counseling allows each partner to put issues on the table once again in a fresh, clear manner. Disconnected from the emotions and history surrounding the relationship, a therapist or adviser can ask questions that neither partner could ask, and in addition, a therapist can listen fairly. A third party with no reason to favor one partner over the other frees the flow of emotion. The therapeutic environment creates a safety net that allows a level of honesty that may have become impossible at home. The therapist can help a couple develop strategies to untangle the knots their relationship is in.

One partner may be ready to seek help before the other is. That's okay. Most counselors will tell you that with or without your partner, seeking help is critical. Of course, once you start seeing someone for help, your partner may very well decide to join you, even if only to have the opportunity to defend herself. That's okay, too. Again, it unlocks a frozen situation and gives your relationship the stimulation that may be its only hope of improvement.

It is a wise and brave decision to acknowledge when you need advice. Far from being shameful, it is evidence of maturity and depth. With help, you can begin to peel away individual issues and deal with them one by one, working toward something new and stronger.

Keep in mind that few problems are one-sided, if any. It takes two people to create the problems in a relationship. If you are committed to therapy, then you've agreed to put your own judgment on the line. It's to your benefit to know where you've gone off-track just as much as to have someone back you up where you haven't.

92.

Articulate Your "Ouches"

You may allow a lot of small irritations to fester in your relationship when you choose to keep your pain—the "ouches" that arise in relation to your partner—to yourself. Maybe you've decided while licking your wounds that your mate's ability to sense your injuries will be the test of whether he really loves you. However, it's childish and unfair to expect a person to "just know."

If you want to keep the small cuts from growing larger, you need to tend to them as you would physical wounds. They need to be looked at, cleaned, and dressed. In a vital, maturing partnership, this leads to better understanding and more compassion for one another. It allows the one who is hurting to lay the pain to rest and get on with living a satisfying life.

The only way to air out your wounds is to verbalize them. Choose your time to speak judiciously. Don't broach the subject of hurt feelings or anger when you're both tired or already emotionally charged for some reason. Find a time when your resources are at their strongest and your mind is at its clearest.

Choose your words carefully. If you frame your conversation in terms that sound like an attack, which is easy enough to do when you're in pain, your partner is likely to throw up his defenses. "You always..." or "You make me..." come from attack modes. If you want to be heard, you need to find ways to communicate that concentrate on your feelings.

Finally, give your partner the opportunity to think about what you've said and respond in his own time. Perhaps he will see justice in what you say and apologize. Regardless of the outcome, resolve to put the pain aside once you've aired it. Forgive and forget. Forgiving allows you to move beyond the hurtful realities in your life. Forgetting allows your wounds to heal.

93.

Resist Humor at Your
Partner's Expense

Humor is a gift. Through humor, we lighten our daily load, gain perspective on our many flaws, and keep from taking things too seriously. The ability to laugh at ourselves moves us toward balanced self-awareness.

But humor can also turn you on your head. What is funny to one person may be deeply offensive to another. What one person may intend as a lighthearted quip may inadvertently touch on another person's pain.

Perhaps most upsetting, however, is humor aimed at a life partner. Many couples develop a pattern of teasing one another in the company of others. Sometimes it's a way to show how well they know one another. Sometimes it's an attempt to avoid actual criticism of their partner, even though what they're communicating is, in fact, critical. Some couples use humor in private, as well, and sometimes to good effect. If you have something serious to say to or about your partner, humor can take the edge off and make it palatable.

In any case, you need to remember that humor—especially teasing—can transform a moment for the better, but it can also be transformed by the moment in which it is heard. What you say in jest may be taken in deadly seriousness. This is true with any other person—especially your life partner.

For example, your partner may make fun of an extended family member in private as a way of coping with unresolved negative feelings. When you do the same in front of others, you suddenly find yourself in trouble. Her negative feelings don't change the fact that the person you're poking fun at is a family member who has played an important role in her life. It's easy to trip over someone else's feelings when you choose to tease.

Always reconsider any joke at your sweetheart's expense. Many jokes at someone else's expense are not received with as much good humor as it may seem. You may be touching on a vulnerability. Go gently, and keep your antennae tuned. Make a point of asking your partner about her feelings related to your teasing at a moment other than when you're joking. If you're going to risk poking fun, *be prepared to apologize* if your joking backfires.

Humor is indeed a gift, but it requires sensitivity, compassion, and self-restraint. In the interest of fair play, if you're going to ask your partner to be the fall guy, you had better be willing to play that role yourself. In fact, if you're determined to make *someone* the butt of a joke, maybe it should be you.

94.

Remember Love

We are at such a disadvantage in modern Western culture when it comes to love. Movies, books, talk shows, sitcoms, articles—all depend on romance, high passion, and unending titillation for ratings and sales. In the process, even nonfiction offerings leave us with the impression that if this isn't present at all times in our relationships, then love itself is absent.

Love as applied to a life partner includes the romance, to be sure, and in fact usually begins with that. But it encompasses so much more. Qualities such as friendship, emotional support, and commitment have an indispensable role in intimate love, as do affection, mutual concern, and a financial pledge of some sort. And under all of these, holding them up, is loyalty.

Loyalty to a life partner illustrates a unique attachment that supersedes all others. Without it, the prerogatives of your bond— sexual, financial, and emotional—become meaningless. You may not be romantic at all times, but you had better be loyal.

Consider the issues that cause friction between you and your mate. Take them one at a time and put them to a test. First, ask yourself if a particular annoyance involves a question of loyalty. For example, a partner might legitimately object to a mate spending the evening with someone else—of the opposite sex, particularly—on the basis of loyalty. No matter what the protestations about how innocent the whole event is, the offended partner will have a valid point based on the demands of loyalty and love.

Ask yourself, too, if an issue, while not specifically related to loyalty, might be answered on the basis of loyalty. Suppose, for instance, that one partner has an obligation to invite an important colleague to dinner who is a notorious bigot. Suppose that the other partner is deeply offended by such bigotry. How does loyalty speak to such a situation? Surely, if you love, it plays a part.

Questions of loyalty are most easily discussed and most quickly resolved when you take the time in untroubled moments to articulate what your bond implies. What does loyalty signify in your partnership? The answer varies from one couple to another, depending on the type of people they are, the levels of confidence they have in one another and themselves, and frankly, what they can tolerate emotionally. Part of loyalty involves honoring a partner's insecurities and needs out of love and compassion for that person.

95.

Believe in the Power of One

"It only takes a spark to get a fire going," goes the old summer camp song. It's true. One spark starts a fire. One remark sets a rumor going. One proud mother gets a whole audience clapping. One worker rallies an entire workforce to raise needed funds for a coworker's surgery. This is the snowball effect. This illustrates the power of one.

When you're discouraged or anxious, you may lose your faith in what one person can do. When you've allied yourself with a life partner, you may come to think that if you're in something alone—that is, your mate won't back you up or get involved—you can't make a difference. You allow yourself to feel defeated, and with that, you often are.

For the most part, we don't appreciate resistance. We would prefer to follow a straight line and encounter a minimum of bumps in the road. Yet most of the remarkable accomplishments in life, global and local, have started with one visionary and scores of detractors. And in a surprising way, the resistance that one person encounters can help to put muscle and intelligence into what is only a small idea at the outset.

The first step in making a difference is knowing that you have the power of one to do so. Without some sense of that, you'll become your own most effective resistance. If you're struggling with defeat, pause and do some research. Look at other people's accomplishments. Talk to others who have experience. Take the time to accumulate the information that you need. There's no substitute for a solid understanding of what it will take to do what you hope to do.

Remember that you only have to take a step at a time. Looking too long and hard at all that may be involved loses its positive value if you don't then break it down into small increments of change. One step leads to another, and the effort will accumulate. Like a snowball, your project will grow as it gains momentum.

Finally, you need to see the project through. The outcome may be less than you hoped, or it may exceed your wildest dreams. But unless you stay with it to the end, you are sure to be disappointed, and you will have missed much of the value your character and self-esteem can gain by staying the course.

96.

Go Mountain Climbing

It is important to learn to climb above your daily problems to keep them from taking over your life and dispelling your joy. They aren't going to go away. For every small irritation you pluck from your life, two are likely to grow in its place. They will litter the landscape of your life like so much underbrush in the foothills of a great mountain range. You cannot change that. But the mountain goat has something to teach us.

The mountain goat climbs daily upon the highest ground, far above the cares and concerns of the average critter. It travels on sure feet over terrain that looks impossible. It roots out vegetation and uses it for nourishment. It discovers rivulets fed by melting snow and quenches its thirst. It accomplishes all this through small, individual decisions, making only one move until it can seek out another.

We have a penchant for quick fixes. We've been taught to expect them by society. But life doesn't often cooperate. The more you try to take giant steps forward, the more you may trip over your own strides. Now consider the goat. It patiently works its way up a cliff face, moving one step at a time. It doesn't seem to concern itself with the long drop or the terrifying view. It simply moves steadily forward. Remarkably, it eventually reaches the summit in one piece.

Learn from the mountain goat. Rather than trying to take a giant leap over the minor irritations and frustrations of daily living, stop and deliberate. Think about your possible next steps. Remember that it takes only a small increment to move you forward. Find that step and take it.

When you feel as though you no longer have the energy to take the next step, remember that life almost always offers sources of replenishment along the way. You have daily opportunities to nourish your mind and spirit and to quench your emotional needs. Looking for the quick fix or the great leap only gets you in trouble. Slow and steady progress, with regular pauses to refresh yourself, can carry you to new heights.

97.

Delete the Negative

Language can be a powerful force. When you inflate negative language, it can become the centerpiece of your interpersonal communication. Every small matter between you can become food for negative thought. But negativity is a habit, and habits can be broken.

Behavior experts claim that it takes six weeks to break or make a habit. If you begin now, you can establish a new, positive pattern of thinking and relating in a month and a half. That's a relatively short span of time in relation to a lifetime—and the benefits are hard to beat.

First of all, notice negativity. Perhaps it begins with friendly teasing. It's all in good fun, but there's enough truth behind it that it begins to stick. Before you know it, the negative has taken hold. So pay attention to conversation with your mate. Notice the ways that you pick on one another, even in fun. Catch the moments when you choose to criticize rather than support.

You may feel discouraged by the extent to which your partnership dwells on the downside. Let your observations become your tutorial for change. Think constructively: "How can I communicate this in positive terms instead of negative?" "What is good in this situation, and how can I emphasize it?"

Now, rather than simply trying to expunge what you no longer want, you are replacing it. A computer image comes to mind. A computer has only so much capacity at any given time. You can be rattling along and suddenly see a message on your screen that indicates insufficient memory to continue. You have to delete something old to make room for something new. If you want to program positive support attitudes into your relationship, you need to delete the negative by replacing it with the positive.

Anything small that is rooted in a negative attitude has a way of growing if you let it—but so, too, does that rooted in the positive. Once you plant it, feed it with a conscious effort to express the upside in your relationship. It can change your attitude and your reality. Emphasis on what is good encourages more good to grow.